ARTILLERY OF WORDS

By the same author:

A BIBLIOGRAPHY OF THE WORKS
OF SIR WINSTON CHURCHILL

YOUNG WINSTON'S WARS

ARTILLERY OF WORDS

THE WRITINGS OF
SIR WINSTON CHURCHILL

BY
FREDERICK WOODS

LEO COOPER
LONDON

First published in Great Britain in 1992 by
LEO COOPER
190 Shaftesbury Avenue, London WC2H 8JL
an imprint of
Pen & Sword Books Ltd.,
47 Church Street, Barnsley, S. Yorks S70 2AS

A CIP catalogue record for this book is available
from the British Library

ISBN 085052 298 6

Typeset by Yorkshire Web, Barnsley, South Yorkshire
in Linotron Times 10½ point

Printed in Great Britain by
Redwood Press Limited
Melksham
Wiltshire

CONTENTS

For Nicky

'Give me the facts, and I will twist them the
way I want to suit my argument.'

SIR WINSTON CHURCHILL

ACKNOWLEDGEMENTS

I must express my gratitude to the Churchill Estate for permission to quote from copyright works; and to Anthea Morton-Saner for her hard work in settling the many problems involved.

I must also thank Dr Desmond Flower and Dr Martin Gilbert for their early encouragement, and for making my studies possible; Trevor Jones for his unobtrusive but stimulating guidance; Dr E.F. Slade for his understanding forbearance; Margaret Bird for expert help in Keele University Library; Councillor Peter Nurse for his unselfish efforts on my behalf; Leo Cooper and Tom Hartman for everything (and more) that good publishers do; Michael Wybrow for his free book service; and last but not least, the University of Keele for accepting me.

And, above all, to Nicky, for her unfailing support and constancy.

PREFACE

As a matter of course, I have used throughout the first editions of
Churchill's works. Two exceptions, however, should be noted: for
Marlborough I used the 1947 two-volume edition (the text is
unchanged), and for *The Second World War* I used the first English
edition; although the American edition claims precedence, it only
contrived this by premature publication, and the text is by no means
Churchill's final version.

INTRODUCTION

Sir Winston Churchill published fifty books, one hundred and fifty pamphlets, well over eight hundred feature articles and three short stories; he contributed forewords, introductions and articles to eighty-three other books, wrote a film script, supplied notes to a series of jigsaw puzzles about famous battles and had twenty long-play and thirty short-play records to his credit.

Both his sales and his earnings ran into millions. Few authors in the history of serious literature can have sold more copies or earned more money. He received the Nobel Prize for Literature in 1953.

Sir Winston Churchill was only a part-time author.

In 1906, with six books already behind him, the young Churchill addressed the annual dinner of the Authors' Club as follows:

'Authors are the happy people in the world, whose work is pleasure. No one can set himself to the writing of a page of English composition without feeling a real pleasure in the medium in which he works, the flexibility and the profoundness of his noble mother tongue. It is a privilege to sit at a table on a sunny morning and feel that there are four hours of uninterrupted security, with plenty of white paper and a pen, away from the vexations of daily life. What does it matter to a man in that position what goes on outside his study door? The House of Commons may do what it likes, and so may the House of Lords; the American market may have its bottom knocked out; the heathen may rage in every part of the globe; Consols may fall, and the suffragists rise; but the author is secure as almost no other man is secure... I have sometimes fortified myself amid the vexations, vicissitudes and uncertainties of political life by the reflection that I might find a secure line of retreat on the pleasant, peaceful and fertile country of the pen, where one need never be idle or dull.' [1]

An idyllic picture of the writer's life. Probably not Churchill's, however, because already his writing life was a lot more pugnacious than those of his audience. A good dinner, some good wines, an excellent cigar, a civilised ambience, a cultured audience, all these would have sparked in Churchill a vision of a literary 'sunlit upland'. The view is essentially an escapist one, happily ignorant of the sheer struggle of writing to make a living. By 1906 Churchill was already well launched upon his career and his view of the writer's life can only have been tailored for his audience. If there was one thing that he was not, it was a writer whose only pleasure was the sheer joy of writing.

In spite of his words, Churchill was never the writer in the ivory tower. Maybe he felt that vision as a subliminal tug, but for him writing was always a much more practical matter. His speech gives an altogether too placid picture of authorship as far as he was concerned, and I cannot believe that he felt any envy for those few whose lives might have been like that.

So if, in spite of his loving description of the writer's life, he was not that sort of writer, what sort of writer *was* he?

In the year in which Churchill won the Nobel Prize, the then Managing Editor of the *Daily Telegraph,* Sir Colin Coote, wrote: 'Churchill is certainly the King of the freelances, but he is not a professional'.[2] It is difficult to see, even from the context, precisely how Sir Colin was using the world 'professional'. In one sense it is clearly inapt, as Churchill was in his day the most highly paid writer in the history of British journalism. The statement is, therefore, presumably pejorative, implying that Churchill failed to achieve certain unspecified standards; as such it is a prime example of the curious general reluctance to grant him professional status in any field except politics.

One can also cite Professor J.H. Plumb's edgy judgment: 'In those fields where his work challenges comparison with professional history, Churchill remains, by the most generous assessment, a gifted amateur.'[3] It is further significant that, when Churchill was made Royal Academician Extraordinary, specific mention was made of his 'amateur' standing.

The British are, of course, as notoriously suspicious of polymath brilliance as they are of popular success: to demonstrate the former merely evokes the phrase 'master of none', while to achieve the latter is to sacrifice all hope of serious consideration. And Churchill was a successful and brilliant polymath; what was worse was that he was an autodidactic polymath, which is even more suspect.

Quality was discernible in his writing as early as 1898, when his despatches from the Sudan showed a sudden maturing of an already noticeable gift. Recognition was almost immediate and continued throughout his long and varied life. Small wonder, then, that there have been instinctive reactions against such a blatantly multi-stranded record of success.

Certainly a blindly adulatory attitude towards Churchill does him no service whatsoever. Criticism is not only possible, it is essential. The truth inevitably lies somewhere between the heady acclaim of the wartime and immediately postwar years and the unyielding denigration that has too often opposed it. And this is as true of his writing as it is of his painting, his politics and his oratory.

From the first precocious but remarkable war books to the bravura swan-song of his *History of the English Speaking Peoples,* Churchill's literary career seems to be studded with brilliant achievements, record sales and lavish fees. But no author, particularly one whose life-span was so considerable and who had so many other preoccupations, can maintain a totally unblemished level of creation. To recognize this in considering the works of Sir Winston Churchill is to take the first step towards a true appraisal of his literary status.

Quite so; unfortunately, it isn't quite as uncomplicated as all that. If it were, judgment would be relatively simple. One would examine and assess the progress of his literary style, his linguistic skills and (though with circumspection) his public reputation and sales performance. And, if one wished to be fashionable, his structures (though with even more circumspection!)

But Churchill was never a pure writer — if, indeed, such an animal has ever existed. He was a writer in whom the man, the life, the beliefs, the prejudices were of paramount importance; and one must treat his writings almost as *oeuvres à clef* from which the truth cannot be found without first uncovering the motivation behind each one.

To a varying degree, of course, this is true of many writers. Can one assess *Seven Pillars of Wisdom* without a detailed knowledge of T.E. Lawrence's complex and self-tortured life, and of the Mesopotamian campaign? Can one judge, to cite two widely disparate examples, *Villette* or *The Ballad of Reading Gaol* without knowing the personal backgrounds involved? Indeed, dare we even evaluate such contemporary historians as A.J.P. Taylor and Hugh Trevor-Roper without first knowing their quirks and foibles, their favourite axes in need of grinding? Or even Thucydides, Caesar and Clarendon? Or, possibly ironically, even the first Sir Winston Churchill?

If this is true of the foregoing authors, it is doubly true of Churchill, since all his books and many of his Press articles were written with ulterior motives. These were inevitably various, but one can say that the broad underlying impetus was propaganda. Even his novel *Savrola* was at least partially a statement of his political beliefs at the time, immature though those doubtless were.

In the following pages I shall examine Churchill's writings from this point of view and, at the same time, show how his quickly-learned professionalism (*pace* Sir Colin Coote) and the unique method of composition that he evolved could turn an advocacy into an onslaught which was capable, when required, of being escalated into a major and sustained campaign.

I shall also incidentally look at the way in which he was supported by the publishing world, the critics and the public — supported to a remarkable degree for an avowedly polemical author. Normally the British do not like being preached at, but in his case, in spite of his years of *political* ostracism, the public seems to have enjoyed the process, providing him not only with an effective platform but also frequently astonishing sales figures.

From the early 1930s on (though one can actually justify a much earlier date) one of Churchill's main platforms was peace. In view of this, it is perhaps ironic that he should have received the Nobel Prize for Literature, an award normally restricted to creative writing. While he wrote some major — even possibly classic — books, the Peace Prize would have been much more appropriate; though, of course, his not-so-transient reputation as a warmonger (with which I shall deal later on) stood in the way of that more accurate honour.

Given that Churchill regarded his books as weapons, it is probably not surprising that he also gives the impression of not being greatly interested in books *per se,* though perhaps this is an over-statement. In spite of his addiction to and self-education through such writers as Gibbon and Macaulay, he seems to have known little of literature of any kind for most of his life. Violet Bonham Carter has related, in *Winston Churchill as I Knew Him,* how he reacted to some famous lines by Keats.

'Later on he asked me whether I thought that words had a magic and a music quite independent of their meaning. I said I certainly thought so, and I quoted as a classic though familiar instance the first lines that came into my head:

"Charm'd magic casements, opening on the foam
Of perilous seas, in faery lands forlorn..."
His eyes blazed with excitement. "Say that again," he said, "say it again — it is marvellous." "But," I objected, "you know these lines. You know the 'Ode to a Nightingale'." He had apparently never read it and never heard of it before...

'Finding that he liked poetry I quoted to him from one of my own favourite poets, Blake. He listened avidly, repeating some lines to himself with varying emphases and stresses, then added meditatively: "I never knew that that old Admiral had found time to write so much good poetry".'

Although that quotation relates to his earlier years (1906), Lord Moran encountered similar ignorance during the 1950s. Only in 1953, according to Moran, did Churchill discover Trollope, followed by the Brontës, Scott, Hardy and some lesser authors such as C.S. Forester, Margaret Irwin, Georgette Heyer and Francis Brett Young. After his self-cramming days in India, books do not feature much in his correspondence or, it seems, in his life. [4]

He had, to be sure, a facility for quotations (though he did not always get them right) which tended to create an impression of being well-read. He also had the undoubted facility of being able to gut a book with remarkable and single-minded speed. Whilst always alive to the power of words and capable of responding with real appreciation to both prose and poetry, his actual knowledge was surprisingly patchy for one popularly considered to be a leading stylist.

But then, as I have proposed, Churchill was not a truly literary author, and if, as he observed in 1898, 'the balance between Imports & Exports must be maintained', then presumably he found all the fuel he needed in the books he specifically chose to consult.

Churchill entered the gladiatorial arena with his very first appearances in print and to the end of his days never forsook it. He was not always the one to stand over his fallen opponent and demand the thumbs down, but he was always a crafty and doughty protagonist; and he survived, he survived.

I

BEGINNINGS

WHEN young Winston Churchill left Harrow in 1893 there was little in his achievements to suggest the future Prime Minister, historian, biographer, essayist, journalist, novelist — and gladiator. At his three schools he had left behind a record of slovenliness, inaccuracy, untidiness and sheer laziness that culminated in his failing to secure sufficiently high marks in the Sandhurst Preliminary Examination to permit him to take a commission in the infantry. Lord Randolph, who had done little if anything to assert paternal authority in the preceding years, exploded to his mother, the Duchess of Marlborough:

> 'He has gone got himself into the cavalry who are always 2nd rate performers in the examination and which will cost me £200 a year more than the infantry wld have cost. I have often told you & you never would believe me that he has little [claim] to cleverness, to knowledge or any capacity for settled work. He has great talent for show off & make believe. In all his three examinations he has made to me statements of his performance which have never been borne out by results. Nothing has been spared on him; the best coaches every kind of amusement & kindness especially from you & more than any boy of his position is entitled to. The whole result of this has been either at Harrow or at Eton to prove his total worthlessness as a scholar or a conscientious worker. He need not expect much from me.'[1]

From the very beginning, his school work had given cause for worry. His report on writing and spelling from St. George's School, Ascot, for the period 3 November-9 December, 1882, was: 'Writing good but so slow — spelling weak'. By the following July this had deteriorated to: 'Spelling about as bad as it well can be'. And the next year, at the Brighton school run by the Misses Thompson his

6

first report on English subjects was: 'Marks gained 1341; Highest gained 6031; Position in class 11; No. in class 11.' And by way of increasing the irony that subsequent events have added, he was also bottom in classics and drawing.

Although he improved his position in class to fourth, he was still reluctant to concentrate. After only three months at Harrow, his form master H.O.D. Davidson wrote to Lady Randolph despairingly, 'his forgetfulness, carelessness, unpunctuality and irregularity in every way, have really been so serious that I write to ask you when he is at home to speak very gravely to him on the subject....Winston, I am sorry to say, has if anything got worse as the term passed. Constantly late for school, losing his books, and papers and various other things into which I need not enter − he is so regular in his irregularity that I really don't know what to do; and sometimes I think that he cannot help it'.[2]

Admittedly, after this rather pathetic complaint, Davidson relented and added: 'He is a remarkable boy in many ways, and it would be a thousand pities if such good abilities were made useless by habitual negligence. I ought not to close without telling you that I am very much pleased with some history work he has done for me.'

So at least his first compliment for work could be classified as prophetic, but for the rest Churchill was, as he admitted himself later, a poor and lazy scholar. At the end of his time at Harrow, after three years in the Army Class, he failed his Sandhurst Preliminary at the first attempt, and at the second failed to get into the infantry by eighteen marks. His father, having angrily dashed off the letter to the Duchess, turned his attention to his son four days later in a letter that is notable for its calculated harshness.

'With all the advantages you had, with all the abilities which you foolishly think yourself to possess and which some of your relations claim for you, with all the efforts that have been made to make your life easy & agreeable & your work neither oppressive or distasteful, this is the grand result that you come up among the 2nd rate and 3rd rate class who are only good enough for commissions in a cavalry regiment....

'I am certain that if you cannot prevent yourself from leading the idle useless unprofitable life you have had during your schooldays and later months, you will become a mere social wastrel, one of the hundreds of the public school failures, and you will degenerate into a shabby, unhappy & futile existence.'[3]

In the face of this diatribe, it is small wonder that Churchill ruefully (and with an impressively controlled understatement) observed to his mother: 'He seems awfully displeased with me'.

And yet, only two years later, Churchill started his professional writing career. It seems extraordinary that this potential 'social wastrel' could turn so quickly and so thoroughly into one of the most famous — and certainly one of the highest paid — writers of the twentieth century; a writer whose capacity for extended work was prodigious, and whose scholarly standards were by no means negligible; a writer whose existence was as far removed as possible from being 'shabby, unhappy and futile'.

There must have been signs, of course; and so there were. But not many, and those few mere hints that probably only hindsight can distinguish. For although Churchill attended one of the major British public schools, his education was sadly lacking when the time came to leave, particularly in those subjects that make up what is usually described as 'a liberal education'. There are few references in his letters to any of the arts. On 4 October, 1886, at the age of eleven, he wrote home that a Mr Beaumont had given a lecture on Shakespeare's *Julius Caesar* — 'an old man,' he added condescendingly, 'but read magnificently'. In the same month there is the suspiciously deadpan statement: 'We are learning Paradise Lost for Elocution, it is very nice.' Many other boys have felt similarly uninspired by a too-early encounter with Milton's endless lines, and it is scarcely surprising to find Churchill saying in 1950, 'My advice to the young is not to read [the classics] too soon'. Predictably, he was more enthusiastic over Rider Haggard (to the point of insisting on being taken to meet him) but in spite of a request for copies of *She* and *Jess* on 24 June, 1887, he was still without them at the beginning of October when he wrote whimsically to his mother, 'I am afraid you have forgotten all about "She". If you knew how much I was longing for "Her", I am sure you would send her to me.'

But in the same letter is the first indication of literary ideas.

'I am thinking of trying to write a little Play, and as you proposed, we might act it at Christmas.

'It would employ my "Leisure Hour" with an at once amusing and useful occupation. If you think it is practicable, say so, and I'll try my hand on a "Comedy".'[4]

Personally, I view this sudden enthusiasm for writing with a certain wariness. The letter is both too carefully written and uncharacteristically 'good'; there is a little too much of the Lord Fauntleroy about that well-behaved phrase 'an at once amusing and useful occupation'. At his age, and in the context of his normal pursuits at school, he should have viewed useful occupations in his leisure hour in the same way that Just William viewed useful presents at Christmas. But however that may be, the play was apparently never completed. In the middle of November he was still at work on it, and mentioned it in a letter home dated conjecturally 13 December. Next day, though, the blow fell.

'Dearest Mother,
    Miss Thompson told me of your plans before your letter arrived. I am very disappointed at hearing that I must spend my holidays without you.'[5]

In spite of all this, Churchill's interest in drama persisted for a while. Having received a pound in Christmas presents he bought himself a model theatre in which he later put on productions at school.

'Please ask Everest [his nurse] to send down all the things and Scenes connected with the play "Aladdin" and the stage as soon as the 5 trap doors are made.
    'Also please send me a bottle of Sperm oil for the 8 footlights. I am very ambitious to beat the others.'[6]

On a more educational level, Churchill took the part of Martine in a Christmas performance of *Le Médecin Malgré Lui* and appeared with another boy in an extract from Aristophanes' *The Knights* ('I think it will prove very amusing to all')
    Another early hint, only fulfilled towards the end of his life, was his request for a copy of Grant's *History of the American War* as a birthday present.
    But, as might be expected, these were more examples of boyish enthusiasm than indications of things to come. So far as we know, he had produced nothing up to this point; it was at Harrow that the creative processes started to work, and here, in his first essay in May, 1888, there were visible one or two small inklings of the Churchillian style. The subject was 'Palestine in the time of John the Baptist', and it opened with a geographical résumé.

'At the time of John the Baptist Palestine's physical features were the same as they are now – The even coast line with its only projection of any importance, Mt Carmel, forms the Eastern boundary of the Levant.

A range of mountains running parrallel [sic] to the coast, East of which the country slopes down to a depth of several hundred feet below the level of the sea — The river Jordan which passes through the Lake of Gennesareth & the Dead Sea. So shall they be till hoary Time be merged into boundless Eternity.'[7]

In later years Churchill would have got the rhythm of the last sentence more accurately balanced, with a monosyllable instead of 'boundless', but certainly the sonority is unmistakable. And later, when he turns to discuss the Pharisees, he wrote:

'Their faults were many. Whose faults are few? For let him with all the advantages of Christianity avouch that they are more wicked than himself, *he* commits the same crime of which he is just denouncing *them*. To sum up their faults *briefly* yes *briefly* — (we do not wish to dwell upon the failings of others for that is not Christian) we may set the chief down as follows:-

'Their hypocrisy.

'Their idea that all, who were not *as good* as themselves, were cursed for ever more.

'Their self-pride and self-Justification. These formed their principle [sic] faults.

'Now *I* think that having mentioned peoples faults we ought to mention their excuses. When we think that for nearly 800 years their [sic] had been no prophet & consequently they attributed this absence of a protector to the "not keeping of the Law". Thereafter they enforced it all the more rigorously, adding & enlarging on it every year until the Public were hemmed in a Perfect network of sinister [?] and worthless laws which to the poorer classes became at once more onerous & impossible to obey. Those who did not obey the law were "outcasts" & "sinners" & they were excluded from the pale of religious & Eternal life.'[8]

This is endearingly funny but it is possible, I think, to discern tones of voice at once familiar and nostalgic.

'Their faults were many. Whose faults are few?' The brief, balanced sentences, the opposition of statement and rhetorical question, the very rhythm could equally well be found in a speech of 1940. And who cannot hear the Churchillian delivery in them, see the left arm extended in a visible question?

From this point, Churchill's lasting interests began to assert themselves. In the examinations during December, 1890, his essay subject was 'The American Civil War'. One of the subjects he rejected was 'Advertisements — their use and abuse'; ironically, topics like this provided a good proportion of his income during the 1930s: 'Life — the greatest secret of all', 'Great deeds that gave us our Empire' and even 'Are there men in the moon?'

Although he retained his interest in the theatre into old age (doubtless encouraged by his daughter Sarah), his appreciation during his youth was somewhat less serious. His only recorded visits to the theatre at this time were to see *HMS Pinafore* during January, 1888, and another visit which seems to have caused passing difficulties with his headmaster.

> 'Darling Mummy,
>
> 'Welldon wants you to write to him and "explain" why I did not come back Thursday. "The Doctor's Certificate" says he "accounts for Wed." I told the animal I understood that if you telegraphed, it was sufficient. "Nay" saith he. But *I* see, and *he* says he does not want to make a row. So he proposes that you should write him a letter saying that I was unable to "favour him with my prescence" on account of --- anything. Twiggez-vous?
>
> 'Don't say anything about the Theatre or that would make him rampant.'[9]

So might the letter, one is tempted to observe. It is undeniably crisp, rapidly-moving, and imbued with a rude vigour in more senses than one. However, though Churchill was not above abusing his headmaster behind his back, he was certainly ready to come out fighting in the school magazine, *The Harrovian*, to which he wrote a number of letters under the pen-names of 'De Profundis', 'Junius Junior' and 'Truth'. The *noms-de-plume* were not a result of any desire to hide his light (never a strong desire in him at any time) but more an adoption of the then current practice when writing to the Press; and in any case it is difficult in the closed society of a school to remain anonymous if others do not wish you to do so. Churchill could have had no illusions on that score.

And here, for the first time, the gladiator enters the arena — not, to be sure, with a firm military stride so much as with a hop, skip and a jump. He was untrained, and his weapons were the bludgeon and the mace rather than the stabbing trident or (in later terms of weaponry) the teasing rapier. But the pugnacity was unmistakable, so much so that the fledgling warrior was uncompromisingly slapped down by his elders. Fortunately or unfortunately, he never quite absorbed the lesson, and though in his later years he learned to annihilate with greater subtlety, he could still return − even during the Second World War − to schoolboy levels of abuse. The 'Schickelgruber' gibe is just one example.[10]

That, however, lay in the future. For a moment, let us examine the infant gladiator, clad in shining if minuscule armour, for here surely were the beginnings of the Great Combat.

His first published letter ('De Profundis') was short and uncontroversial, merely suggesting revised opening times for the Vaughan Library. His second under that name was not published, and attacked working conditions in certain parts of the school where 'the free wind of heaven has free access from every quarter'. Then in December, 1891, came the first of his 'Junius Junior' letters, in which he castigated the failure of any Harrovians to appear in the school Assault-at-Arms (Corps Field Day). The answer, by one 'Aequitas Junior', appeared two months later, and immediately the Churchill of Question Time made himself felt.

> 'I had to read his letter several times before I could determine whether it was intended for an answer or a confirmation of what I wrote. But since it explains the one sentence of my letter he is good enough to quote, I have decided to consider it as an answer.
>
> 'I will not pause to criticise his style, nor comment on his probable motives, though I am inclined to think that both are equally poor....'[11]

Not surprisingly, the editors of *The Harrovian* omitted part of the letter which, they said, 'seemed to us to exceed the limits of fair criticism'.

After this exchange, Churchill concentrated on gossip-column letters, composed of brief chatty paragraphs on school affairs.

Lightweight these letters may have been, but we meet at once − and surely it is not mere hindsight that tells us so − a stripling Churchill suddenly in command of his case and his language. Or, to express it another way, a Churchill knowing and relishing his weapons.

One of the letters concerned the number of towels in the school gymnasium. He puts the case in four devastating sentences:

> 'i. The room possesses two towels at present.
> ii. These are changed once a week.

iii. They are used during that time by over 300 boys.

iv. Gymnastics is conducive to warmth.'[12]

One can only admire the restraint of the final line, even while reflecting that at Harrow cleanliness appears to have been a fair distance from anything, let alone godliness. It is pleasant, though, to be able to record that some sort of success attended Churchill's efforts. On 15 June he could claim:

> 'The number of towels has been increased to *four* per week. It is reported that the outlay and *great* expense of this improvement will be met in part by a grant from the School Funds and in part by voluntary subscription from the friend of the Gymnasium.'[13]

The word 'friend' is not a misprint for 'friends', so apparently Churchill was not sanguine about the amount that would be raised. Or is it a suddenly adult sarcasm?

So, by the time he left Harrow, Churchill had proved himself to be an adept recruit to controversy, and if it is true that much of the controversy was carried on at a very schoolboyish level, it is equally and regrettably true that much Parliamentary controversy is carried on in precisely the same vein.

II

SELF-EDUCATION
AND THE EARLY CAMPAIGNS

AT the beginning of September, 1893, Churchill joined the Royal Military College, Sandhurst. During his training, there is little mention of reading other than purely military works, but he developed a taste for theatre-going; it was, in fact, this taste that produced his first appearance in public print, in the *Westminster Gazette* of 19 October, 1894. His letter, headed 'The Plimsoll Line in Respectability', sought to instil moderation into the bitter campaign against the Empire Theatre, led by the improbably named Mrs Ormiston Chant.[1] While Churchill's sympathies were entirely with the supporters of the Empire cause (and not for the last time, either), he tried – unsuccessfully – to bring democratic processes to bear upon the problem. Privately, in a letter to Mrs John Leslie, he commented sourly, 'It is hard to say whether one dislikes the prudes or the weak-minded creatures who listen to them most. Both are to me extremely detestable.'[2]

But in spite of his concentration upon his career and the frivolity of his leisure hours, Churchill was now genuinely concerned about the many gaps in his education. When his mother suggested to him that he should study the problem of the supply of army horses, he protested that he needed something more literary and less material. Everything he had read previously, he pointed out, was aimed at passing examinations and had not imparted the polish that he would have received at Oxford or Cambridge. And he went on, presumably to his mother's incredulity, 'I have now got a capital book – causing much thought – and of great interest. It is a work on political economy by Fawcett... [*Manual of Political Economy* by Henry Fawcett, 1863.]

'Then I am going to read Gibbon's *Decline and Fall of the Roman Empire* and Lecky's *European Morals*. These will be tasks more agreeable than the mere piling up of shoppy statistics.'[3]

So began the dogged self-education that continued for several years, and particularly during his period of service in India. He read largely from curiosity, without any informed help, with the result that in spite of prodigious knowledge in certain fields, he remained remarkably uninformed and even naive in others. He was, for instance, as Violet Bonham Carter found out some years later, almost totally ignorant of poetry. His reading of creative literature generally was patchy, and remained so to the end. Of music he knew virtually nothing, and painting meant little to him until he came to paint himself. But from being a boy whose spelling was 'about as bad it well can be' he became in his early twenties one of the most widely read and admired war correspondents in the history of British journalism, worthy of taking his place alongside William Howard Russell and G.W. Steevens; and the inclusion of his description of the cavalry charge at Omdurman in an anthology of classic war literature in 1942 was no empty gesture by its editor, that *aficionado* of war Ernest Hemingway.

Having passed out of Sandhurst and been gazetted into the 4th Hussars, Churchill looked around for practical experience. Unfortunately for him, the world was at peace just then, with the exception of an insurrection in Cuba where guerrillas were harassing the Spanish army under Marshal Martinez Campos. Rebellion had been simmering since 1868 and, after a relatively peaceful period, a slump in sugar prices in 1893-4 triggered off new risings. Campos, with 200 officers and 7000 men, was still trying to put the rising down.

Churchill, whose regiment was preparing for a nine years' stint in India, was due for leave. Funds were low as he had recently spent more than he should on polo ponies, and the prospect of seeing war and, at the same time, conserving his resources, appealed much more than the almost obligatory fox-hunting with which he would otherwise have been faced. As he pointed out to his mother, the return ticket would only cost £37, 'which would be less,' he added craftily, 'than a couple of months [hunting] at Leighton Buzzard.' Lady Randolph, in the light of her offhandedness during Churchill's schooldays, reacted perversely. 'I was rather looking forward to our being together & seeing something of you. Remember I only have you & Jack to love me.' But her son was already in characteristic full flow. He persuaded a fellow subaltern, Reggie Barnes, to go with him, and received permission from his Commanding Officer, Colonel Brabazon. He also wrote for letters of introduction to his father's old friend, Sir Henry Drummond Wolff, now conveniently the British Ambassador in Madrid.

Throughout his army service Churchill never hesitated to go straight to the top, either personally or through his mother; the habit was not universally admired. Having arranged the introductions through Madrid, he went to no less a person than the Commander-in Chief, Lord Wolseley, for final approval. Wolseley approved of the venture in a rather oblique way, passing Churchill and Barnes on to the Director of Military Intelligence, who supplied them with maps and general information, and asked them to collect intelligence in their turn.

At the same time, remembering that his father had written for the *Daily Graphic* from South Africa in 1891, he approached T. Heath Joyce, the Editor, and arranged to write a series of letters for a fee of five guineas each.

His first despatch appeared in the issue of 13 December, 1895, and opened with a nice blend of self-consciousness and ingenuity.

> 'Most people have probably noticed that the initial difficulties of any undertaking are in many cases the most insuperable. The first few sentences, whether of a proposal of marriage or of a newspaper article, require more thought, and involve more effort, than any of those which follow. And if this is the case with those who are accustomed by experience to break the ice in either circumstance, how much more does it apply to the beginnings of the beginner. It is on account of these difficulties that I shall allow their enumeration to stand in place of further prelude, and plunge at once into the middle of the subject − and the harbour of the City of Havana.'

The remainder of the report is an admirable brief survey of the situation, studded with vivid details, such as the intriguing method used by insurgents for destroying the sugar crops of uncooperative planters: 'A piece of phosphorus, coated with wax, would be the probable instrument of the incendiaries. This little pill is fastened to the tail of the Cuban grass snake, a common and inoffensive creature, which is then let loose. The sun melts the wax and ignites the phosphorus, and the result is a conflagration, without any possible clue as to its authorship.'[4]

While this method of sabotage seems unlikely to endear itself to herpetophiles, it is impossible not to admire the ingenuity of its conception, and it is typical of even the young Churchill that he should have seized upon this detail. One could even wonder whether this encounter bore eventual fruit in the succession of weird and wonderful devices dreamed up by his boffins forty-five years later; except that the British devices were more complex and had a higher failure rate.

Churchill's second despatch appeared in Britain four days later. Written at Sancti Spiritus, 'a forsaken place, and in a most unhealthy state,' it is notable for the conclusions that he had reached in a remarkably short space of time. Moving swiftly and surely from farce to high seriousness, he illuminated one of the truths that afterwards brought angry Spanish reactions and upset the even tenor of Sir Henry Drummond Wolff's life.

'It was explained to me that when challenged by any sentry or outpost it was necessary to answer very sharply. If, by a process of deduction which Sherlock Holmes himself might envy, you arrive at the conclusion that the outpost is Spanish, you answer "Spain"; if, on the other hand, you think it is a rebel post, you reply "Free Cuba"; but if you make a mistake it is likely to be very awkward. The great advantage the insurgents have is the detailed and constant information which they receive. Their only uniform is a badge. This can be taken off at will, and when so removed it is impossible to tell a rebel from an ordinary peasant. Hence they know everything; the position of every general, the destination of every soldier, and what their own spies fail to find out their friends in every village let them know. The more I see of Cuba the more I feel sure that the demand for independence is national and unanimous. The insurgent forces contain the best blood in the island, and can by no possible perversion of the truth be classed as *banditti*. In fact, it is a war, not a rebellion.'[5]

This judgement is particularly interesting in that it directly controverts his conclusion in the first despatch, where he had written: 'The twofold object of the rebels... is to make plain to the entire world the power they have − and so obtain recognition as belligerents from the United States − and by plunging their country into indescribable woe to procure the intervention of some European Power. Looked at from any standpoint, it is a dreadful and a desperate remedy, and one which neither restriction of liberty nor persistent bad government can fully justify.'[6]

Yet, four days later, he distinguishes between a mere rebellion and a justified war. Churchill's war reporting never shrank from the truth, a characteristic that brought him enmity in high places but which also helped to ensure the rapid increase in his public reputation. His cry, 'If I were a Boer, I hope I should be fighting in the field' is probably the best-known example of his unimpeded vision during his early years, but equally so was his outspoken criticism of Kitchener for his handling of the Sudan campaign of 1898.

With singular appropriateness, Churchill came under fire for the first time on his twenty-first birthday. During the afternoon he and Barnes and two Spanish staff officers were surprised while bathing in a river. Shots whistled over their heads but a small counter-attack dealt with a few rebel marksmen and Churchill and his party 'retired along the river as gracefully as might be'. More shots were fired at eleven that night when the fusillade was kept up for about an hour.

> 'This time they employed volleys, and killed and wounded several soldiers about the camp. One bullet came through the thatch of the hut in which we were sleeping and another wounded an orderly just outside — but otherwise we were not affected by the fire.'[7]

Thirty-five years later, as might be expected, he dealt with the episode in a lighter-hearted way.

> 'We dined undisturbed in the verandah, and retired to our hammocks in the little barn. I was soon awakened by firing. Not only shots but volleys resounded through the night. A bullet ripped through the thatch of our hut, another wounded an orderly just outside. I should have been glad to get out of my hammock and lie on the ground. However, as no one else made a move, I thought it more becoming to stay where I was. I fortified myself by dwelling on the fact that the Spanish officer whose hammock was slung between me and the enemy's fire was a man of substantial physique; indeed one might almost have called him fat. I have never been prejudiced against fat men. At any rate I did not grudge this one his meals. Gradually I dropped asleep.'[8]

Churchill's final letter to the *Graphic* was judicious and solid, and did its best to balance the discrepancy of attitude between the first and second letters. Once again, his sense of the ridiculous pointed the report.

> 'Outside the gates of Ciego d'Avilar... a rather curious incident took place. The guard of course recognized the General, but the prescribed forms had to be observed. Word was sent to the Governor that a party of horse had arrived and desired to enter. A long parley, lasting quite

twenty minutes, took place, with the object of making sure we were not wolves in sheep's clothing, and finally the Chief of the Staff was permitted to advance and be examined. The sample proving satisfactory, we went in. This procedure is, I believe, of ancient origin, and is most punctiliously observed. It appears excellent, the only weak point being that the gate was left open and unguarded while it was being carried out.'[9]

Then came the summary and the compromise, though both are lit by Churchill's precocious but accurate political and tactical comments.

'There is no doubt that the island has been overtaxed in a monstrous manner for a considerable period. So much money is withdrawn from the country every year that industries are paralysed and development is impossible. Nor is this all. The entire Administration is corrupt.... Bribery and peculation pervade the boards of works, the post-offices, the Customs, and the courts of justice on a scale almost Chinese. A national and justifiable revolt is the only possible result of such a system.

'But I sympathise with the rebellion − not with the rebels....They will not even submit to military discipline. A friend of Maximo Gomez − a man who had been frequently in his camp − told me the rebel leader confided in him that when he tried to drill the insurgents they immediately asked to be sent home. Is this the stuff out of which nations are made? The only tactics they pursue are those of incendiaries and brigands − burning canefields, shooting from behind hedges, firing into sleeping camps, destroying property, wrecking trains, and throwing dynamite. These are perfectly legitimate in war, no doubt, but they are not the acts on which States are founded....

'Cuba is between Scylla and Charybdis....A compromise alone is possible.

'No one ought to allow himself to be puzzled by the contradictory telegrams or by the glorious victories and crushing defeats which appear daily in the newspapers. Cuban battles are many of them imaginary, most of them exaggerated, and all of them devoid of importance. The one thing to look for is the position of the insurgents. If Maximo Gomez is able to maintain himself in the provinces of Santa Clara and Matanzas till the hot weather he will have gained a decided advantage, and the inevitable compromise will be correspondingly favourable to the autonomist party − and conversely.

'Such is the state of affairs in the richest island in the Spanish main. It may be that as the pages of history are turned brighter fortunes and better times will come to Cuba. It may be that future years will see the island as

19

it would be now, had England never lost it — a Cuba free and prosperous, under just laws and a patriotic administration, throwing open her ports to the commerce of the world, sending her ponies to Hurlingham and her cricketers to Lord's, exchanging the cigars of Havana for the cottons of Lancashire, and the sugars of Matanzas for the cutlery of Sheffield. At least let us hope so.'[10]

This is tightrope walking with a vengeance. In his second letter he had sympathized with the rebels; now he sympathizes with the rebellion but not with the rebels, on the grounds that they are not disciplined. But this could be said of many insurgent forces, particularly when the war they wage concentrates on guerrilla tactics. The rebel tactics he admits to be legitimate in war but denies that states can arise from them; but why on earth can states *not* arise from them? The continued existence of the Castro régime firmly refutes the contention.

His comments on Gomez's position were, of course, clear-sighted and can be paralleled by his appreciation of the tactical situations during the Boer War. Had this country been invaded in 1940, Churchill could well have been a very successful guerrilla leader.

His final paragraph, alas, is hilarious rather than sound; the prospect of a Cuban cricket eleven must have shaken the MCC Committee to its core. More seriously, the rolling phrases — 'a Cuba free and prosperous, under just laws and a patriotic administration' — ring falsely even for the turn of the century. Clichés are clichés, and this example of Churchillian rhetoric surely owes too much to stock attitudes to be convincing.

Nevertheless, minor faults apart, Churchill's Cuban visit was a definite success. He and Barnes were awarded the Spanish Rioja Cruz for gallantry,[11] and in all the Cuban newspapers he appeared, a touch prematurely, as Sir Winston Churchill. Elsewhere, reactions were generally excellent. Both the Duke of Tetuan, the Spanish Minister for Foreign Affairs, and Marshal Campos wrote to Drummond Wolff in cordial terms about their visitor, and on 10 January, 1896, the editor of the *Graphic* wrote as follows:

'I may say that your letters and sketches[12] have been extremely interesting and were just the kind of thing we wanted. I enclose you a cheque for twenty-five guineas for the five letters which is the honorarium of five guineas per letter we agreed upon.'

Four days later the *Graphic's* manager W.L. Thomas, also wrote:

'Allow me to compliment you on the result (as I imagine of your first experiences) as a Special Correspondent & artist combined.

'Your letters were very interesting and to the point and the sketches useful in adding point to the letter press and I am sorry that your time was so limited and so preventing your sending more.

'In spite of recent events attracting public attention in other directions,[13] your letters were widely read and appreciated.'

Another letter, however, brought news of Spanish displeasure. On 17 February, 1896, Wolff wrote from Madrid:

'Please read the enclosed which is attributed to you. I should be very glad if you could avoid saying things unpalatable to the Spaniards; having obtained the letters on your behalf which secured your good treatment I am reproached for the unfavourable commentaries you make.

'I am sure you will be careful as this kind of thing places me here in a painful dilemma.'

Fortunately an article written by Churchill for the *Saturday Review*[14] soothed the ruffled Spanish feelings and Wolff was able to write:

'Many thanks for your letter and telegram. I have shown them in the proper quarters but they were no longer required as your article in the *Saturday Review* has been translated in all the papers and has created much enthusiasm.'

Meanwhile Lady Randolph had been working behind the scenes again, distributing copies of the despatches to key people. In a letter dated 3 March, Joseph Chamberlain described them as 'The best short account I have seen of the problems with which the Spaniards have to deal, and [it] agrees with my own conclusions derived from informants in the United States and in Spain. It is evident that Mr Winston kept his eyes open.'

So ended Churchill's first experience of professional journalism, a small and not very significant beginning to what was to turn into a career that would net him the highest fees ever offered. A small mark had been made, the next step awaited. But it had to wait until the following year, when Churchill's regiment finally moved to India. Only an abortive attempt at another journalistic expedition marked the year. One of Crete's occasional periods of unrest prompted him to offer his services to the *Daily Chronicle*. Although he was refused, he cannot have been too displeased with the tone of the refusal sent by the paper's Assistant Editor, Henry Norman.

> 'I have been talking over your proposal with the Editor, and he agrees with me that it would not be possible, under the circumstances I explained to you when I first mentioned the matter, for us to ask you to proceed to Crete as our Special Correspondent. At the same time, however, if you decide to go, we should be very glad to avail ourselves of your assistance. If you should visit the points of the island which are now attracting such prominent attention and should find the material for, say, five letters of about a column and a half each, we would be willing to pay you for such Correspondence at the rate of ten guineas a letter.
>
> 'I may add that if you were able to send us any news of great importance, or to secure any facts or descriptions of sensational interest, we should be very ready to increase those terms considerably.'[15]

For a young man of only twenty-one, this must have been — should have been — flattering indeed. In the event Churchill did not go to Crete but rejoined his regiment to start on the next stage of not only his military but also his literary career. His first venture in the field of journalism was also the last that showed a financial loss.

The importance of the Cuban letters is slight — a passing glance at a minor conflict. But they showed clearly that, even as a newly-fledged subaltern, he was not afraid to judge and utter on military matters. His fighting instincts were still largely untried, but they were there, and in the next few years they would bring him both trouble and the beginnings of lasting fame.

Churchill could only see his going to India as 'useless and unprofitable exile'. Instead he wanted to go to South Africa and then on to Egypt (largely for the medals), but these plans had to be postponed, and on 11 September, 1896, he sailed on *SS Britannia* with the 4th Hussars. At Bangalore his worst fears were justified; the routine was hardly energetic. Up at 5 a.m. for a light snack before parade at 6, breakfast and a bath at 8, stables between 9.45 and 10.45, and then nothing till polo at 4.15, mess at 8 and then bed. Faced with that sort of regimen, a young subaltern could succumb to boredom and apathy, and many did; but Churchill's restless mind came to his aid. He grew roses, and gathered an impressive butterfly collection with interest and flair, vengefully hunting down and killing the rat that destroyed it. More to the point, he began to fulfil his ambition for a liberal education, and his chosen reading was diverse. With his brother Jack he did not feel the need to impress and could discuss lighter types of literature than were ever mentioned to his mother. The following letter is interesting not only for its judgments, but also for its discussion of the problems of being a best-selling author − a problem that was to beset Churchill himself.

'Rudyard Kipling's new book [*The Seven Seas*] is I think very inferior and not up to the standard of his other works. Few writers stand the test of success. Rider Haggard −Weyman −Boldrewood are all losing or have already lost their prowess. What happens is this. An author toils away & has many failures. Rejected contributions − books which the publishers won't publish − accumulate. Money does not. One day he writes a book which makes him famous: *King Solomon's Mines, A Gentleman of France* or *Robbery under Arms*. His name is now on everyone's lips − his books are clamoured for by the public. Out come all the old inferior productions from their receptacles, and his financial fortune is made. Few authors are rich men. Few human beings are insensible to the value of money. If a book by Weyman is worth a £1000 to him, that book will be written. Hurried style − exaggerated mannerisms & plagiarisms replace the old careful toil. The author writes no more for fame but for wealth. Consequently his books become inferior. All this is very sad but true − and I am afraid Kipling is killed.'[16]

Churchill's own earnings were, in time, to make those of Haggard and Weyman, even of Kipling, look niggardly and the presence of the bottom drawer became noticeable in his life too.

However, light reading apart, Churchill was working steadily, partly for self-improvement, partly as an anodyne against boredom.

'Poked away in a garrison town which resembles a 3rd rate watering place, out of season & without the sea, with lots of routine work and a hot and trying sun − without society or good sport − half my friends on leave and the other half ill − my life here would be intolerable were it not for the consolation of literature....Notwithstanding all this, I have not been unhappy, though occasionally very bored, and I contemplate without repugnance returning to my books, my butterflies & my roses.'[17]

In March, 1897, he reported that he had read or was reading Macaulay, Gibbon, Winwood Reade's *The Martyrdom of Man,*

Laing's *Modern Science and Modern Thought,* Jowett's translation of Plato's *Republic,* Rochefort's *Memoirs,* Gibbon's *Life and Memoirs* and one volume of the *Annual Register.* At the same time he asked to be sent the *Memoirs* of the Duc de St Simon and Pascal's *Provincial Letters.*

> 'I find my literary tastes growing day by day — and if only I knew Latin and Greek — I think I would leave the army and try to take my degree in History, Philosophy and Economics. But I cannot face parsing & Latin prose again.'[18]

Gibbon and Macaulay were, of course, his literary gods, whose influence stayed with him all his life until the full-blown phrase became second nature. Indeed, at the time when he was absorbing the full impact of these authors, he showed little signs of their effect in his writing. A touch of reaction shows itself in the comment: 'I suppress with difficulty an impulse to become sententious. Gibbon and Macaulay, however much they may improve one's composition of essays or reports, do not lend themselves to letter-writing.' To Jack he brushed away criticism with a refusal to discuss that possibly argues a certain sheepishness.

> 'I am sorry you don't appreciate or approve of my literary style. Gibbon in his autobiography says, "The habits of correct writing may produce without labour or design the appearance of art and study." That excuse is good enough for me and I hope you will be graciously pleased to accept it.'[19]

To read Macaulay and Gibbon simultaneously in the heat of an Indian afternoon is an impressive piece of self-discipline. Churchill tackled fifty pages of Macaulay and twenty-five of Gibbon every day, as well as other works. Hallam's *Constitutional History* and Adam Smith's *Wealth of Nations* are mentioned, as well as his uncle Moreton Frewen's[20] book on bimetallism, though this discovery of another author in the family was to have dire results. And apart from all this reading, he was going through all the *Annual Registers* he could acquire, first of all deciding his attitude to each Bill presented and then reading the debate.

But writing and the desire to taste war again were close to the surface, and when, in April, 1897, trouble erupted between Greece and Turkey, he set the wheels in motion for his appointment as a special correspondent. With engaging frankness, he discussed with his mother which side he should join.

> 'Of course my sympathies are entirely with the Greeks, but on the other hand the Turks are bound to win....If I go on this side it will be less glorious but much more safe & as I have no wish to be involved in the confusion of a defeated army my idea is that they would be more suitable. You must decide. If you can get me good letters to the Turks – to the Turks I will go. If to the Greeks, to the Greeks.'[21]

Churchill then went on to lay down instructions for his mother as to what arrangements she should make for him. 'I should expect to be paid £10 to £15 an article – customary rate for telegrams but would bear my own expenses. Lord Rothschild would be the person to arrange this for me as he knows everyone. I should recommend Mackenzie Wallace [*The Times*] – Borthwick [*Morning Post*] or failing everything else the *D. Graphic* who would I am sure be delighted. These arrangements I leave to you and I hope when I arrive at Brindisi I shall find the whole thing cut and dried.'[22]

Lady Randolph may have had her faults, but certainly she was required to work – and work hard – to further her son's career. On this occasion she was also required to transfer £50 either to Constantinople or Athens, depending on which letters she could arrange.

This particular conflict fizzled out, but not before Churchill had conceived his first book. He mentioned it to his mother with embarrassed levity: 'When I come back from Turkey I hope to have material enough for a book – so indispensable nowadays to write a book. If you don't you expose yourself to dangerous notoriety. The man who has travelled and never written a book! Shocking!'[23]

Was this embarrassment caused by memories of his father's harsh judgments? Was this expensive, unprofitable child going to write a *book*? There may have been something of this sort in Churchill's mind, for the reference to his plans is uncharacteristically diffident.

Nevertheless, if this particular book was denied to him, he turned to other outlets, and on 24 August, 1897, he made his first reference to his novel *Savrola,* which was eventually published in 1900. With Winstonian (or, possibly, to Lady Randolph, unWinstonian) doggedness, he worked at this on and off for the next two years, laying it aside several times to write his war despatches and histories but always regretting the delays. In fact, it was only five days after his first announcement that he wrote: 'The novel is indefinitely shelved. Five chapters are already completed and I am very much pleased with them.'

The reason for the shelving was the Pathan revolt on the North-West Frontier. At once Churchill wrote to Sir Bindon Blood asking for a place on his staff. Blood's staff was made up, but it was suggested he would get the first vacancy if he went up as a war correspondent. At once Churchill organized his mother and set off without waiting for arrangements to be made. Lady Randolph started at the top, as usual; but *The Times* had already appointed a correspondent, so it was the *Daily Telegraph* that supplied his credentials. At the same time, he himself arranged terms with the Allahabad *Pioneer Mail*.

On 5 September, 1897, he wrote to his mother:

> 'Herewith 2 letters for the *D.T.* I do not know what terms you have made with them − but it should certainly not be less than £10 per letter. Having read please forward − and decide whether they should be signed or not. I am myself very much in favour of signing − as otherwise I get no credit for the letters. It may help me politically to come before the public in this way.'

Clearly, from this last remark, even these early despatches were regarded by their author as a means to a long-term end: political eminence. Already, at the age of twenty-two, his writings had become conscious tools − weapons with which he intended to forge himself an independent career in his father's footsteps. The views he expressed in them were deliberately calculated to draw attention to him, even if that reaction were to prove hostile. All publicity is good publicity, as the saying goes.

Churchill's instructions regarding payment were too late. He should have known by then that business acumen was not his mother's strongest suit. 'I have no doubt,' she wrote airily, 'if you get a chance of sending any [letters] that they will be well paid − of course they must be attractive.' The delays of sea-mail created obvious problems in communication, and before this letter arrived Churchill had sent two more letters for onward transmission to the *Telegraph*. 'Use your own discretion in editing it − as I am too tired to write more now and then post it off. No fighting at present − but possibilities every moment. No ice − no soda − intense heat − but still a delightful experience.'

The blow fell a month later, when Lady Randolph's letter informed him that the *Telegraph* had only offered £5 a column.

However, his mother naively added, 'I have just bought a *D.T.* of today & see another letter which they seem to have cut in two − if they do that there will be more letters & you will get your £10.'

Churchill erupted.

'I will not accept less than £10 a letter and I shall return any cheque for a less sum. I particularly asked for that amount *au moins* and when I think of the circumstances under wh those letters were written, on the ground in a tent temperature 115° or after a long day's action or by a light which it was dangerous to use lest it drew fire...I think they are cheap at the price. The £75 which the *D.T.* propose to give me will hardly pay my ticket for self & horses. The *D. Chronicle* offered me ten pounds a letter to go to Crete and I will not be defrauded in this way. As Dr Johnson says, "Noone but a blockhead ever wrote except for money".[24]

'Will you kindly ask Moreton Frewen if he will go and see the Editor & point out that such a sum is ridiculous and that it is nothing less than a fraud. Correspondents from the theatre of war who pay their own expenses − are entitled to special rates for copy. I will not take less than £150 for the series.'[25]

But for all his fury Churchill did not get his £10 a letter. Any profit that he made came from his subsequent book *The Story of the Malakand Field Force* (1898) which he started to write in November. Meanwhile he continued with his despatches to the *Telegraph,* of which fifteen were published between 6 October and 6 December, 1897, headed 'The War in the Indian Highlands: By a Young Officer.'

The despatches are crisp and authoritative, completely devoid of the verbosity that later began to creep into his prose, when the rhetorical requirements of hustings and Commons affected both his written and spoken styles. Naturally the requirements of field journalism afforded their own tight discipline, and Churchill both observed this and was stimulated by it. Time and time again he conjured up a scene by the economical use of a few words, a small bright particular vision that illuminates the report and lifts it from the mundane to the vivid. Sometimes it is an episode, sometimes a personal reaction, sometimes the most fleeting observation that turns an abstract action into an affair of men, individuals who spring to life even though they remain nameless.

Even before he reached the Frontier, his alert mind relished the following obscure transport problem: 'Long trains of transport show the incessant passage of supplies to the front. One in particular, of camels, presents a striking picture. Six or seven of these animals are crowded into an open truck. Their knees are bound to prevent them moving on the journey, and their long necks, which rise in a cluster in the middle, have a strange and ridiculous aspect. Sometimes, I am told, curiosity, or ambition, or restlessness, or some other cause induces a camel to break his bonds and stand up, and as there are several tunnels in the line, the spectacle of a headless "oont" is sometimes to be seen when the train arrives at Rawalpindi.'[26]

Similarly, in a later despatch, he provides a vignette made memorable by the final speculation.

'I saw a strange thing happen while the firing was going on, which may amuse those who take an interest in the habits and development of animals. Just in front of my tent, which was open, was a clear space, occupied by a flock of goats and sheep. The brilliant moonlight made everything plainly visible. Every time that a bullet whistled over them or struck the ground near them they ducked and bobbed in evident terror. An officer, who also noticed this, told me it was the first time they had been under fire; and I have been wondering ever since whether this explains their fear or makes it more inexplicable.'[27]

But his impact rested not only on sharpness of vision and vividness of phrase. It also rested on his ability to stir up the sort of reaction in high quarters that lesser writers merely dream of. Only Russell, in his despatches from the Crimea, produced similar outrage and resentment, but he achieved more in positive results. Churchill, though he failed to activate any of his proposed reforms, nevertheless gained a wide audience — and a deep and damaging enmity — in both War Office and Parliament with his political comments and recommendations. His youth and lowly rank he ignored; he was on the spot, he believed in his own study and experience, and he was never one to remain silent when he had something to say. On this occasion, with only a few months' service to his credit, a few days' action and no Indian dialect, he had much to say and, in his usual way, went at his probable critics head-on.

'It is fashionable in English politics to discredit the opinion of people on the spot. They are supposed to be excited and prejudiced, to be unable to take the judicial and comprehensive views which can, it is believed, be adopted only in an atmosphere of ignorant indifference.'[28]

Later on, he proceeded to the problems of training and leadership.

'We subalterns in British cavalry regiments do occasionally manage to see a little active service in strange and various capacities – as transport officers or on the staff; but to lead in the field the men we have trained in peace is a possibility which is never worth contemplating....I would suggest that the subalterns should, with the approval of their Colonel, be attached to the native regiment, and, after passing in Hindustani and being reported as qualified to serve with native troops, be considered available for employment as described. I shall be told there are financial difficulties. I do not believe this. There are plenty of cavalry subalterns whose eagerness to see service is so strong that to have an extra chance they would submit to any arrangement that the rapacity of Government might impose.

'To be technical is a grave offence, and I realise keenly that if these letters ever obtained so evil a reputation they would be shunned as the House of Commons is shunned on a service night.'[29]

Such temerity was not to be tolerated and Churchill found himself the recipient of a certain amount of victimization by the Staff. Of course he knew full well what he was doing and, in fact, delighted in the rumpus he was creating. To his old friend Reggie Barnes he wrote: 'I have written a scorcher against the Indian govt to the *D.T.* and later on my letters on the military muddle will make them snort.' Indeed, his main aim in being a correspondent at this time was two-fold, and neither was motivated by the desire to write *per se*. One was the burning desire to see action and secure campaign medals; and the other was to be noticed politically, so that when he came home his reputation would precede him sufficiently for him to be offered a good seat. So his pained surprise when enmity became personally directed was really too good to be true. Indeed, if one wished to be malicious, one could observe that it is a poor gladiator who bursts into tears on being hit back! After such criticism on the part of an obscure subaltern, it is scarcely astonishing that the subaltern in question might find it difficult to get the staff position he coveted. Churchill, however, did not see it this way, and wrote to his mother in injured self-pity.

'The Simla authorities have been very disagreeable indeed to me. They did all they could to get me sent down to my regiment and refused to have anything to say to my being appointed to my post. I hear also that they all talked about me very much and said they would take good care I got nothing out of it and was not attached to the force....I will invite you to consider what a contemptible position it is for high military officers to assume − to devote so much time and energy to harrying an insignificant subaltern....Talk to the Prince [of Wales] about it.'[30]

Throughout his life Churchill used whatever friends and acquaintances he knew who were in positions of power, and at this early stage in his life, he was lucky enough to number the Prince of Wales among them. The relationship was not always plain sailing; often the Prince put his foot down on some particular piece of Churchillian recklessness and was constantly advising him to act more prudently. For the most part Churchill heeded his counsel and remained the loyal and humble servant, and on this occasion he did not press his cry for royal help. Perhaps he eventually realized that he probably deserved what he got, and, in any case, what he got was a small price for the immediate response that his despatches drew at home. This was not wholly due to brilliance, it was also due to the memory of his father, and his mother's tireless proselytizing among the wealthy, the nobly born and the politically influential. His old headmaster, perhaps, did not fall into any of these categories, but his reaction of 22 October, 1897, must have gratified Churchill enormously, providing as it did a perfect rebuttal to his father's sweeping condemnation of the boy at Harrow. 'I think he possesses in a high degree the special correspondent's art of seeing the picturesque and interesting features of a campaign. Really he is very clever, and must make a mark in the world.'

Being at such a distance, Churchill did not immediately know the response to his words; he did not need to, for, without waiting, his mind was made up. On 10 November, 1897, he laid aside his novel, now in its eleventh chapter and 'progressing capitally' and announced his determination 'to write an account of the whole campaign in book form to be called "The Story of the Malakand Field Force", which is to be dedicated to Sir B.B. There is a good deal of material. The political questions alone are very wide. The attack on the Malakand and the relief of Chakdara...will have to be added to the account of the operations I witnessed myself....It is a great undertaking but if carried out will yield substantial results in every way, financially, politically, and even, though do I care a damn, militarily.'

To an extent, of course, the book would merely be a case of

working from his existing despatches. But there were the other actions to be drawn into the account, about which he did not have first-hand information. He solved this in a way that foreshadowed his eventual methods with startling similarity. 'I have written to all the colonels and knowledgeable people I met up there for facts etc. and I do not doubt I shall receive volumes by return of post. Such is the modesty of the age. Few people are above saying what really happened from their point of view. Of course I shall have to discriminate.'

He was to use this technique both in the Sudan and South Africa (though he ran into trouble with Kitchener in the former campaign), and it later blossomed into the impressive teams of professional researchers, advisers and assistants.

From that point on, his whole life was wrapped up in the book. He was working on it for over eight hours a day – 'and astonish myself by my industry and application' – and was under no illusions about his achievement: 'I am producing a fine piece of English.' He was equally certain that his mother would like the style, 'which is of a wide compass from an easy conversational account to most stately periods.' Needless to say, even while he was still in the early stages of composition, and alarmed by the news that the *Times* correspondent, Lord Fincastle, was also preparing a book on the campaign, he chivvied his mother into acting once again as unpaid agent and propagandist.

> 'I want you to find out from Sampson and Low whether they would be willing to publish for me. Of course they cannot say until they have seen. But I have asked Major Hobday – a most skilful artist who witnessed all the operations – to illustrate it and I want to find out some details as to what the usual division of profit between author & artist should be.'[31]

Lady Randolph, having her own methods of organizing other people which were just as effective as her son's, passed the problem on to Arthur Balfour who recommended his own agent, A.P. Watt.

Meanwhile the work of writing, editing and revising went on with relentless efficiency. The original *Daily Telegraph* letters were broken up and reworked, amplifications made, judgments reconsidered, and new material – arriving by every post – incorporated. 'I have broken up the *D.T.* letters completely – you will recognise only parts of them. Most is entirely rewritten. I am ambitious – though of course the haste with which the book has

31

been constructed militates against it − of something better than Railway bookstalls.' And then, with rare humility: 'However I daresay I take inflated views of everything.'[32]

Two weeks later he wrote again to his mother.

'A fortnight from today I shall, if the fates are propitious, send you *The Story of the Malakand Field Force* an Episode of Frontier War by Winston S. Churchill. I hope you will like it. I am pleased with it chiefly because I have discovered a great power of application which I did not think I possessed. For two months I have worked not less than five hours a day and had I more time I should like to take another three or four months and produce something of value as well as of interest. I will write you a covering letter with the MS explaining my views on the subject of its publication. But it should be worth a good deal of money. This we cannot afford to throw away.'[33]

It was, in fact, only nine days later when the promised covering letter was sent. As it shows the remarkable degree of planning which Churchill brought to his first publication I quote it in full.

'My dearest Mamma,

'Herewith the book. It has by a great effort been finished a week earlier than I expected. Maps and a photograph of Sir Bindon Blood for frontispiece, I hope by next mail, but do not delay publication on their account.

'I have hurried vy much & it is possible there are still a few slips and errors of writing in the MS. I cannot have the proofs sent out here as that would take too much time. I want you therefore to ask Moreton Frewen if he will undertake the work of revising and correcting them for me. I shall be vy grateful indeed if he will. I enclose some notes as to publication & as to the points I want whoever revises to look out for.

'Failing Moreton − Ivor Guest and failing him do find someone − well read and clever. I do not see why you should not do it yourself − but proof correcting is a great labour and involves many technicalities and conventional signs. Moreton would be best of all and I am sure he would do it for me.

'Now dearest Mamma I don't want anything modified or turned down in any way. I will stand or fall by what I have written. I only want bad sentences polished & any repetitions of phrase or fact weeded out. I have regarded time as the most important element. Do not I beg you − lose one single day − in taking the MS to some publisher. Fincastle's book may for all I know be ready now.

32

'As to price. I have no idea what the book is worth but don't throw it away. A little money is always worth having. I should recommend Moreton's treating with the publishers, it is so much easier for a man. If the book runs to a second edition, I shall add another three or four chapters on Buner which is now impending. I have wired Blood to take me again on this new advance. I do not expect to go. Allow nothing to prevent publication of this book. I have taken great pains − nor do I think the result altogether unworthy.

'I have gone to the expense of sending this by letter post in order to save the week of sea journey. So I beg you do not lose time. I don't think I ought to get less than £300 for the first edition with some royalty on each copy − but if the book hits the mark I might get much more.

'No more my dear Mamma. Believe me I am weary of the pen. No letter from England at all for me this week. But I look forward to your next. Write and tell me all about the book and wire me result of any bargain you may make. You need only say the price & then the royalty and the probable date of publication. My last words, like the bishop's, are "verify my quotations."

'Ever your loving son,
Winston'

'*Notes for Revision and as to Publication*

'I have regarded Time as the most essential point. Do not send MS here, but print from your corrections. I have thought of the book as a *cheap and popular* work − but I will bow to publishers wishes in this respect. I do not recommend pictures unless accurate. Many in illustrated papers are ridiculous. (Maps − see separate note.) Cover: Title and cover − with Salisbury's quotation in right hand bottom corner − should be as I have suggested. (But again I would give way if thought unsuitable.) Printing: I attach greatest importance to a large & clear print. The work is not a long one and needs spacing. Headings: I suggest before each chapter some suitable headings for the pages. I think that style more suitable to the tone of writing. Should an appropriate one occur and the spacing need an extra heading I shall be grateful if you will have it inserted. Time is the most important factor. To publish while interest is keen & before others write (I hear several books are on the stocks) is I am convinced most necessary.

Points as to the MS
Will you kindly look out for:
a. awkward sentences
b. repetitions
c. Division into paragraphs

d. Uniform spelling. It is possible the clerks may have spelled the same name differently. I enclose a list of some of the names and words about which there may be a doubt.
e. Words omitted.
   I have revised MS but some omissions may have escaped me.
And last *Please verify my quotations*. I have very few books here. (Note. Chapters 7, 8, 9, not yet decided on, sending by next.)
Maps: I have procured and am sending.
1. Map of Mamund Valley"
    To face chapter XI
2. Map of Nawagai & strategic situation
    17th Sept - 25th (Chapter XIII)
3. Plan of attack upon Agrah. Chapter XIV
4. Plan of Malakand" Chapter IV
5. Two cavalry actions (insert at discretion)
    a. chapter V
    b. chapter VI
I want publishers to procure
1. Map of N.W. Frontier"
2. Map of Chitral road
Of these " are essential.'[34]

Letters flowed to Lady Randolph throughout January, 1898, cajoling, instructing, commanding, wheedling − and at times returning to the still-rankling matter of the *Daily Telegraph* fees. 'Stingy pinchers,' he growled in a return to the classroom. 'You ought to have stuck out for a tenner, or sold them elsewhere. It is no good being too high and mighty over business matters. All men meet on equal terms and the labourer is worthy of his hire.'[35]
On 19 January he fired off another long letter full of instructions, but accepting with relish the incidental opportunity for another dig at the *Telegraph*.

   'You must see that all efforts are made to launch it well. Reviews & editorial notes must be arranged & carefully worked up. It ought to have some circulation in America − and this should be carefully looked to. I made it my business to lunch with the Editor of the *Pioneer* at Calcutta and he will do all he can out here. (By the way he would not believe the *D.T.* had the conscience to pay me so little for the letters. He said they were a paper noted for their meanness.)
   2. I must repeat again − *"Verify my quotations"* particularly the date of Ld Salisbury's Guildhall speech. I am not sure it was "1892"...'

34

Like so many authors approaching the time of labour, Churchill was already excitedly discussing his offspring's future, even though no acceptance had yet reached him. On 26 January he wrote to his mother:

'The publication of the book will certainly be the most noteworthy act of my life. Up to date (of course). By its reception — I shall measure the chances of any possible success in the world. Although on a larger subject and with more time I am capable of a purer and more easy style and of more deeply considered views — yet it is a sample of my mental cast. If it goes down well then all may be well.'

To Lady Randolph this would not have seemed to be tempting providence, as she had received an offer six days previously. A.P. Watt had sold the book to Longmans, Green — 'on terms,' wrote Watt in a not very elegant phrase, 'which I have no hesitation in advising you are such as you may with entire confidence accept.' The terms were, in fact, generous for a first book, the basic royalty being half as much again as that agreed decades later as adequate by the Society of Authors. The offer was a royalty of 15% on a selling price of 6/- (30p) for the first three thousand, rising to 20% thereafter; threepence (1½p) per copy for the Colonial Library edition; 10% for the first thousand copies sold in America, rising to 15% thereafter; and an advance, payable on publication, of £50.

After a swift calculation that this would probably bring him in about £300, Lady Randolph closed with the offer and Longmans proceeded to typesetting and mapmaking with such speed that she received the first batch of proofs only seven days after A.P. Watt had informed her of the offer. To her son she wrote:

'I have written to Buckle, Frank Harris — & Norman — asking them to review yr book favourably when it appears, which will be in a fortnight or so, *so* expeditious have Longmans been....Sir D. Mackenzie Wallace tells me that Longmans as a rule only publish at the cost of the author, & that in itself is a compliment. Arthur Balfour only got £200 down for his book I believe — & owing to royalties he has made up to now £3000. If your book sells you will make a good deal....If the book is a success — & I am sure it will be — you can command yr own price next time.'[36]

By the same post Churchill received a letter from the Prince of Wales, whose friendly warning, for once, arrived too late: 'Your mother...tells me that you are bringing out a book with an account of your recent campaign which I shall look forward to read — as you have great facility in writing — which is a great advantage. I only hope you will be prudent in your remarks — & shun all acrid criticisms which would be received by the Authorities'.[37]

Like most authors, Churchill had an attack of cold feet after acceptance —'it seems vy bald and stale and futile and fulfils vy little the high hopes with which I embarked on the enterprise' — but it was out of his hands, and Longmans, if they did not act with quite the expedition that Lady Randolph imagined, published the book on 14 March, 1898, having increased the price in the meantime to 7/6 (37½p). Two thousand copies were printed for the home market, together with a similar amount for the Colonial edition. Within six months a further 1500 copies were ordered for the Colonial Library, and these were run off with an equal quantity for the cheap Silver Library edition which appeared in the following year; and in January, 1899, a final 1500 were run, 500 for the Colonial edition, and 1000 for the Silver Library.

These were respectable figures for a first book about an obscure and minor frontier campaign, and there is little doubt that they would have been considerably larger had it not been for the editorial work of Moreton Frewen. Precisely *what* he did is unclear, beyond the fact that he changed Churchill's punctuation — often casual but perfectly functional — to his own, which was, to be kind, eccentric. Precisely *how much* he did is equally unclear, but, whatever it was, it necessitated 122 hours' work by the typesetters in the way of proof correction. And when the book was subsequently reviewed in *The Atheneum* it was described as 'in style a volume by Disraeli revised by a mad printer's reader....One word is printed for another, sentences are defaced by shameful blunders, and sentence after sentence ruined by the punctuation of an idiot or of a schoolboy in the lowest form.'

Years later, when he wrote *My Early Life* in 1930, Churchill commented with a mildness that hindsight allows us to see was misleading: 'I had entrusted their [the proofs'] correction to an uncle of mine, a very brilliant man and himself a ready writer. For some reason or other he missed many scores of shocking misprints and made no attempt to organise the punctuation.' At the time, however, Churchillian rages thundered from distant India, and it is perhaps as well that he and Frewen were so efficiently separated.

Nevertheless, in spite of these shortcomings, the book was an immediate success, and the Prince of Wales wrote in glowing terms: 'I cannot resist writing a few lines to congratulate you on the success of your book. I have read it with the greatest possible interest and I think the descriptions and the language generally excellent. Everybody is reading it, and I only hear it spoken of with praise.'

The Times, too, weighed in with measured phrases, observing that 'the power of direct expression, the unhesitating candour, and the sense of humour displayed by the young author will be noted as a striking instance of heredity.'

Other influential people, however, had very different reactions, as Churchill found out only a few months later.

III

THE LATER CAMPAIGNS

IN 1885 General Gordon was killed at Khartoum, but it was not until 1896 that Britain set out to avenge his death and resubjugate the Sudan. Affairs had gone on in a leisurely manner and were just coming to a head by the time Churchill found himself free to look around again. At first his endeavours to join the punitive expedition were fruitless; the last person Kitchener wanted in his force was the young subaltern whose recent despatches had ruffled so many military feathers. Even when the Adjutant-General, Sir Evelyn Wood, cabled: 'Personage [the Prince of Wales] asked me personally desires you take Churchill', Kitchener stood firm.

Fortunately for Churchill, another powerful ally joined him at this point. At the beginning of July, 1898, he received a summons to meet the Prime Minister, Lord Salisbury, who had just read *The Story of the Malakand Field Force*. Salisbury's enthusiasm knew no bounds. 'I have been keenly interested in your book. I have read it with the greatest pleasure and, if I may say so, with admiration not only for its matter but for its style....I myself have been able to form a truer picture of the kind of fighting that has been going on in these frontier valleys from your writings than from any other documents which it has been my duty to read....If there is anything at any time that I can do which would be of assistance to you, pray do not fail to let me know.'[1]

The next move was obvious and this time Kitchener gave in, but with an ill grace, attaching Churchill as a supernumerary lieutenant to the 21st Lancers on 23 July. 'It is understood that you will proceed at your own expense and that in the event of your being killed or wounded in the impending operations, or for any other reason, no charge of any kind will fall on British Army Funds.'

Among Churchill's earlier salvoes had been a singularly naive cable from Lady Jeune, a well known society hostess, to Kitchener:

'Hope you will take Churchill. Guarantee he wont write.'[2] If Churchill had ever felt himself bound by this proxy undertaking, he quickly took steps to circumvent any responsibility in that direction by arranging with Oliver Borthwick that he would send letters back from the front. Ostensibly these would be private letters which would find their way into print only because the recipient found them so brilliant that he could not restrain himself from passing them on to the *Morning Post*. The fact that Borthwick was the proprietor of that paper went more than a little way towards ensuring the success of the plan.

During the campaign, Churchill sent fifteen long despatches back, each in the form of a letter, with a fictitious explanation of 'provenance' at its head. They remained unsigned, though Churchill's attitude to this anonymity fluctuated. On 11 August, 1898, he wrote to his friend Aylmer Haldane. 'If you look in the *Morning Post* it is possible that you will see that one of my friends has committed and continues to commit an unpardonable breach of confidence by publishing letters of mine. Don't give away the pious fraud as I do not want to be recalled...;' but on 17 September he wrote to his mother, 'There need be no secret about my having written the letters.'

Before the campaign ended, however, Churchill had finally decided to quit the army and therefore had no qualms about signing the last letter in the series. Kitchener was incensed, not only by the bare fact that Churchill had been writing against his express wishes, but also at the personal criticisms contained in the despatches, and, later, to a much greater degree, in *The River War*.

But by the time Kitchener discovered all this Churchill was on his way back to India to tidy up his affairs, and was already writing his considered history of the expedition. On 11 December, 1898, he wrote to his mother from Aden: 'Three very long chapters are now almost entirely completed. The chapter describing the fall of Khartoum Gordon's death etc is I think quite the most lofty passage I have ever written.' By the time he reached Bangalore he wrote again, in words that may have sent anticipatory shivers down his mother's spine.

'The book grows in bitterness about K. I feel that in spite of my intention it will be evident that no friend has written it. I expect they had just about enough of him when he went back to his Soudan. A vulgar common man — without much of the non-brutal elements in his composition.'

A few days later he wrote again, drawing her attention to a

particularly splendid phrase he had just written – a sentence which stayed with him all his life and which is still considered to be one of the most revealing sentences he ever uttered. 'Let me quote one sentence – it is about the Mahdi who was left while still quite young an orphan. "Solitary trees, if they grow at all, grow strong; and a boy deprived of a father's care often develops, if he escapes the perils of youth, an independence and a vigour of thought which may restore in after life the heavy loss of early days." '[3]

Did Lady Randolph, I wonder, see the personal application? On her past form it would seem doubtful.

In March Churchill set off on his return to England, stopping off at Cairo to collect more information for his book. By the end of August it was finished and Churchill paid his debts by writing to Lord Salisbury with an offer of the dedication. Three thousand copies of the book appeared on 6 November, 1899, in two imposing volumes, quickly followed by a further 1000.

Reactions were mixed. As far as can be ascertained, the Prince of Wales maintained a discreet silence, merely acknowledging receipt of his copy. He had expressed himself forcibly during the publication of the despatches however. 'I fear in matters of discipline in the army I may be considered old-fashioned – & I must say that I think that an officer serving in a campaign should not write letters for newspapers or express strong opinions of how the operations were carried out.

'If the Sirdar, as you say, viewed your joining his Force with dislike – it is I am sure merely because he knows you write, for which he has the greatest objection I understand – & I cannot help agreeing with him.'[4]

Others, including Lord Salisbury, General Sir Evelyn Wood and Lord Wolseley were more enthusiastic, as was the *Daily Mail:* 'It is an astonishing triumph...and we do not think any other living man could have produced it.' The *Saturday Review,* on the other hand, expressed the latter phrase in a somewhat different way: 'Only this astonishing young man could have written these two ponderous and pretentious volumes.' There is, in fact, some truth in both these attitudes.

'An astonishing triumph' – 'ponderous and pretentious volumes.' Certainly the book in its original form was overlong, and equally certainly it contained some gems of pretentiousness and padding. Consider, for instance, this description of a railway engine's smoke: 'the malodorous incense of civilisation was offered to the startled gods of Egypt.' *That* sentence did not appear in the original despatches; it occurred when the young writer sat down with leisure to think about 'style' − with some disastrous results.

But, as always, Churchill responded positively and vividly to direct stimuli. Once he was in the thick of the action his eye was sharp and immediate; and his prose reflected that vision − economical, spare, sinewy, fast. His description of the 21st Lancers' charge is accepted as a classic of its kind, and rightly so. It remains one of the best examples of modern military writing.

But there is a great deal more about both the *Morning Post* despatches and *The River War* than just sharp observation. For the first time Churchill began to develop a breadth of vision, a startling (for its time) range of understanding and awareness, and a generosity of spirit that was poles apart from the conventional jingoistic British journalism of the period.

During the Battle of Omdurman he conceived a great respect and admiration for the Dervishes, whose courage he found remarkable. (He was later to develop a similar admiration for the Boers and be equally outspoken about it.)

'I have tried to gild war, and to solace myself for the loss of dear and gallant friends, with the thought that a soldier's death for a cause that he believes in will count for much, whatever may be beyond this world. When the soldier of a civilised power is killed in action his limbs are composed and his body is borne by friendly arms reverently to the grave. The wail of the fifes, the roll of the drums, the triumphant words of the Funeral Service, all divest the act of its squalor, and the spectator sympathises with, perhaps almost envies, the comrade who found this honourable exit. But there was nothing *dulce et decorum* about the Dervish dead. Nothing of the dignity of unconquerable manhood. All was filthy corruption. Yet these were as brave men as ever walked the earth. The conviction was borne in on me that their claim beyond the grave in respect of a valiant death was as good as that which any of our country-men could make. The thought may not be original. It may happily be untrue. It was certainly most unwelcome.'[5]

And, at the end of the same despatch, he wrote a richly purple passage of homage to the same enemy, controlled finally into a dying fall that is both impressive and moving.

'So, as the haze of the desert deepened into the gloom of the night and the blurred outlines of the distant hills faded altogether from the view, we rode back to camp − "home to Omdurman," and left the field of

41

battle to its silent occupants. There they lie, those valiant warriors of a false faith and of a fallen domination, their only history preserved by their conquerors, their only monument their bones — and these the drifting sand will bury in a few short years. Three days before I had seen them rise eager, confident, resolved. The roar of their shouting had swelled like the surf on a rocky shore. The flashing of their blades and points had displayed their numbers, their vitality, their ferocity. They were confident in their strength, in the justice of their cause, in the support of their religion. Now only the heaps of corruption in the plain and fugitives dispersed and scattered in the wilderness remained. The terrible machinery of scientific war had done its work. The Dervish host was scattered and destroyed. Their end, however, only anticipates that of the victors, for Time, which laughs at Science, as Science laughs at Valour, will in due course contemptuously brush both combatants away. Yet it may happen in some distant age, when a mighty system of irrigation has changed the desolate plain of Omdurman into a fertile garden, and the mud hovels of the town have given place to the houses, the schools and the theatres of a great metropolis, that the husbandman, turning up a skull amid the luxuriant crop, will sapiently remark: "There was aforetime a battle here." Thus the event will be remembered.'[6]

Given Kitchener's personality and attitudes, Churchill's chivalry must have been galling indeed. But if such honesty offended, there was worse to come. The criticisms of the *Morning Post* letters were relatively mild, and mostly implicit, since their writer could not wish to stimulate too much investigation into his identity. Once free from military discipline, he not only unsheathed his weapons with relish, but used them with accuracy and venom.

The bitterness he mentioned to his mother showed clearly in his comments on the treatment of the Dervish wounded; the criticism of Kitchener is still, for the moment, only indirect, but it is clear and unmistakable.

'Too much has been said and written about the treatment of the Dervish wounded for anyone who attempts to write a comprehensive account to avoid the discussion....The reader may recall that before the attack on the Mahmud's *zeriba* the Sirdar issued orders that the wounded were to be spared. It is scarcely possible to believe that he wished otherwise at Omdurman. It is nevertheless a pity that his former order was not republished to the troops; for I must personally record that there was a very general impression that the fewer the prisoners, the greater would be the satisfaction of the commander. The sentiment that the British soldier is incapable of cruelty is one which never fails to win the meed of popular applause; but there is in fact a considerable proportion of cruel men in every army. The mistaken impression I have alluded to encouraged this class....The result was that there were many wounded Dervishes killed....Many atrocious acts were also perpetrated by the camp-followers....

'Regiments may exult in the part they played. Military experts may draw instruction from the surprising demonstration of the power of modern weapons. But the individual soldier will carry from the field only a very transient satisfaction, and the "glory of Omdurman" will seem to any who may five years hence read this book a very absurd expression.'[7]

If Churchill had lacerated military hides in his Malakand writings, he went even further in *The River War*, excoriating both the theoretical and practical failures of the British strategy at Omdurman.

'The paramount object for the cavalry was the capture of the Khalifa. Examined from any standpoint, but especially from this, the whole pursuit must be called a hopeless failure. On whom does the responsibility lie? Not on the troopers...not on the cavalry leaders...; but upon the Sirdar, and on him alone....

'The utter lack of all combination between the 21st Lancers and Colonel Broadwood's brigade, and the great interval by which these units were divided, prevented the whole cavalry force advancing together as soon as the enemy were in full retreat. The Egyptian cavalry expended their strength in an ineffective direct pursuit at the tail of the Dervish army. The 21st Lancers, having at a heavy cost gained an excellent position on the flank of the line of retreat, found themselves too few to seriously profit by the advantage they had won. The results were unsatisfactory. The retreating Arabs marched from the field almost unmolested; the Khalifa escaped to rally his followers...and the name of Omdurman must be added to that long list of battles in which the victorious army failed to take advantage of their triumph. It will no doubt be urged that an extra cavalry brigade would have caused an extra expenditure of money. I applaud the cheapness of Kitchener's campaigns. But there is no worse extravagance in war than an economy of soldiers.'[8]

Finally, at the end of *The River War*, Churchill unleashed the full power of his artillery in a passage that nowadays would keep a whole litigation of lawyers happy for months on end.

'The General who never spared himself cared little for others. He

43

treated all his men like machines — from the private soldiers whose salutes he disdained, to the superior officers he rigidly controlled. The comrade who had served with him and under him for many years in peace and peril was flung aside incontinently as soon as he ceased to be of use. The Sirdar looked only to men soldiers who could march and fight. The wounded Egyptian, and latterly the wounded British soldier, did not excite his interest, and of all the departments in his army the one neglected was that concerned with the care of the sick and injured... The stern and unpitying spirit of the commander was communicated to his troops, and the victories which marked the progress of the River War were accompanied by acts of barbarity not always justified even by the harsh customs of savage conflict or the fierce and treacherous nature of the Dervish.'[9]

In terms of sophistication and striking power of weaponry, the difference between *The Story of the Malakand Field Force* and *The River War* (and their associated despatches) is as if a primitive army had gone from spears to crossbows in one generation. Churchill had found his gladiatorial feet with amazing speed. Less than three years before, he had offered comments and criticisms on the very minor Cuban insurrection; now he repeated the exercise, but with a greatly enhanced fire-power and a much more sure-footed tactical (even strategical) sense. He had not forgotten the hustings — indeed, that target was always clear in his sights — but he now felt that he could make bigger sorties, more sustained assaults. His confidence was growing apace, and if he had to sacrifice a national hero, so be it. Churchill was on his way towards his goal. The preliminary stage of that campaign would come to fruition in the next few months.

Leaving aside youthful exuberance and visible signs of a continuing search for an individual style, *The River War* still stands as an outstanding example of war literature. Churchill had digested — and digested well — not only the situations that presented themselves to his eyes, but also the whole sweep of military considerations. Kitchener could doubtless have shrugged aside ill-informed criticism; but, as the Indian authorities had discovered, Churchill had done his homework; the criticisms and suggestions were accurate and considered.

The proofs of *The River War* were read by one of Churchill's friends and colleagues, G.W. Steevens, whose reputation as a war correspondent was then almost as great as Churchill's was to become. Steevens, who went to Ladysmith for the *Daily Mail* when Churchill turned down that paper's offer, and died there of enteric fever, offered an immediate judgment, the rightness and sly humour of which must have stung as it encouraged.

> 'The parts of the book I have read appear to me a valuable supplement to the words of G.W. Steevens — and indeed a valuable work altogether. I think it first rate — sound, well got up & put together & full of most illuminating & picturesque touches. The only general criticism I should make is that your philosophic reflections, while generally well expressed, often accurate & sometimes true, are too devilish frequent. If I were you I shd cut the philosopher about January 1898 — giving him perhaps a short innings at the very end. He will only bore people, those who want such reflections can often supply them without assistance.'[10]

For an *ad hoc* judgment, Steevens' words were 'devilish acute'. He was, in fact, a percipient young man. When he was twenty-eight and Churchill only twenty-four he wrote in the *Daily Mail:* 'He has qualities which could make him almost at will a great popular leader, a great journalist or the founder of a great advertising business.' And also: 'It was not possible that a man who has done so much so well at twenty-four would be altogether popular. Enemies he has probably none, but precocious success is not the way to win facile friendship — even when joined with modesty — and Winston Churchill is, outwardly, not modest.'

The River War remains, without question, the primary source for this campaign, and a book that is a pleasure for non-specialists to read. It has occasional touches of pomposity, to be sure, and occasional literary lapses, but it also has humour, wisdom, humanity, honesty, and a vivid immediacy that remains in the memory long after the book is closed and returned to the shelf.

It is also the book in which the young Churchill disclosed for the first time his full arsenal.

All this is interesting and significant enough, that the twenty-five-year-old journalist was prepared to come out with all guns blazing against the Establishment and, particularly, against an admired and very senior military figure.

What is even more interesting and significant is that *not one* of the passages quoted above — nor, indeed, any other really critical passage — appears in the revised one-volume edition of *The River War,* published only three years later. Narrative and action dominate that edition; it is difficult to find any sustained reflective passage throughout its length — about half that of the first edition.

Of course it is possible to argue that such wholesale editing was demanded by the publisher; or that Churchill had finally — if uncharacteristically — heeded the advice of such friends as the Prince of Wales and G.W. Steevens, Neither, however, seems likely.

The reason is at once simpler and more complex. The basic reason for the excisions is that, by the time the shorter edition appeared (1902), Churchill had accomplished his ambition and was an MP. Further, following his father's example, he had already established himself as a speaker on military matters, and his collection of speeches on such topics, entitled *Mr Brodrick's Army,* was only a few months from publication. It was not the time, therefore, for a continuation of the old tactics, any more than it was the time or the occasion further to alienate one who could be of the utmost service to the young Churchill if he so chose.

For Churchill, therefore, there was no advantage to be gained in reprinting the old attacks on Kitchener; and there could be grave disadvantages in doing so.

Sail-trimming? Certainly yes, quite cold-bloodedly so. But then what politician does *not* trim his or her sails as often as is convenient? The attacks had served their purpose; let them go.

But before anyone condemns Churchill for this blatant piece of *post hoc* adjustment, it would be as well to recall two things. The first is that he used his books as weapons, as political tools; not necessarily as models of objective accuracy. And if the deliberate and fully-acknowledged bias of *The World Crisis* and *The Second World War* has its own truth, then it is inevitable that, on occasions, the same technique will have its less honourable side. This is, sadly, one of those occasions.

But secondly, to lighten this reproach, though possibly with an inescapable hint of cynicism, one can quote the last line of Churchill's epigraph to *The Second World War* —forty-five years in the future but nonetheless relevant to the transient antagonism between Kitchener and Churchill: 'In victory — magnanimity'.

As far as Churchill was concerned, he had won, and he was never one to pursue a battle beyond the point of victory. In any case, with his upper-class background, he would scarcely be inclined to harry 'a vulgar common man'.[11]

So, for these various motives, the offensive passages were quietly dropped, and Churchill's progress was once again, even if only negatively, assisted by his literary career.

Churchill's despatches from South Africa and the two resultant volumes *(From London to Ladysmith via Pretoria* and *Ian*

Hamilton's March) mark both the climax and the end of his brief but incandescent career as a war correspondent. Concise, reasoned, provocative, informed, often downright exciting, they confirmed his eminence in the journalistic world and gave notice that a major factual writer had entered the ring.

His involvement with the Boer War started with the Jameson Raid of 1895 which had, to some extent, diverted attention from his Cuban letters. In late 1896 or early 1897 he wrote an analysis of the situation as he saw it. Entitled 'Our Account with the Boers' it remains unpublished except for a brief excerpt in the first volume of the official biography. This quotation, slight though it is, is sufficient to show that his approach to the problem was largely clear in his mind three years before the conflict started.

'Imperial aid must redress the wrongs of the Outlanders; Imperial troops must curb the insolence of the Boers. There must be no half-measures. The forces employed must be strong enough to bear down all opposition from the Transvaal and the Free State; and at the same time to overawe all sympathisers in Cape Colony. There will not be wanting those who will call such a policy unscrupulous. If it is unscrupulous for the people of Great Britain to defend their most vital interests, to extend their protection to their fellow-countrymen in distress and to maintain the integrity of their Empire, "unscrupulous" is a word we shall have to face....Sooner or later, in a righteous cause or a picked quarrel, with the approval of Europe, or in the teeth of Germany, for the sake of our Empire, for the sake of our honour, for the sake of the race, we must fight the Boers.'[12]

Here, already formulated, are the main points reiterated in the early despatches and the books; protection and state aid for the settlers; a sufficiently strong army; the strength and vitality of the Empire; the necessity for force motivated by benevolence. Indeed, many of Churchill's views were rigidly defined before he went to South Africa. Some were to be reinforced; his political solutions, for instance, and his proposals for state assistance and subsidised emigration. Others were to be changed, particularly his views on the Boers themselves, which swung from hatred to admiration almost as soon as he was captured and accorded humane treatment. ('So they were not cruel men, these enemy. That was a great surprise to me.')

However, at the time of drafting that article, the pot had not yet boiled over and there was time, during its simmering, to fit in the campaigns on the North-West Frontier and the Nile. Then, shortly after his return from Egypt, he received a telegram from Alfred Harmsworth inviting him to become the *Daily Mail's* correspondent in South Africa, where open fighting had finally broken out. Churchill had other ideas and contacted his old friend Oliver Borthwick, offering to write for the *Morning Post* instead. The financial return was exceptional for those days; as Churchill wrote in *My Early Life* with justifiable pride: '£250 a month, all expenses paid, entire discretion as to movements and opinions, four months' minimum guarantee of employment — such were the terms; higher, I think, than any previously paid in British journalism to war-correspondents, and certainly attractive to a young man of twenty-four with no responsibilities but to earn his own living.'

So he caught the first boat to South Africa, accompanied by his own commissariat, including six bottles of Vin d'Ay Sec, eighteen of St Emilion, six of light port, six of French vermouth, eighteen of whisky (ten years old), six of brandy (landed 1886) and twelve of Rose's lime juice. Not for nothing had he been involved in three previous campaigns!

Scarcely had he arrived when he was captured. His triumphant return ensured world-wide fame, a certain seat at the next election and an audience agog to see what he would do next. He was even the subject of a music hall song by T.E. Dunville:

> 'You've heard of Winston Churchill —
> This is all I have to say —
> He's the latest and the greatest
> Correspondent of the day.'

But it is certain that, even without the invaluable bonus of his escape, he would have more than consolidated his already strong reputation. As in the Indian mountains, as at Omdurman, he was in his element with that mixture of creation and adventure that he craved. 'Like so many of the greatest men of action,' observed A.L. Rowse in *The English Spirit,* 'like Nelson, darling of the English people, or Napoleon, or Lenin, or for that matter Caesar — with Mr Churchill writing is bound up in action. They are not mutually exclusive activities but complementary, each impulse seeking fulfilment in the other.'

In the Boer War Churchill found his most stimulating period so far. The Indian affair had been too slight and fragmented, Omdurman over too quickly; but here were extended battles, mighty battles, adversities and defeats, heroism and doggedness — all the properties and qualities that go to make up the Churchillian drama. With three campaigns behind him, his criticisms of strategy and of the High Command generally were biting and incontrovertible. Apathetic or inefficient administration was impatiently exposed; even unimaginative chaplains were flayed. If he had offended through precociousness before, here he wrote with the deliberate intention to hurt and to heal, to get things improved, to run the war more efficiently — behaviour he was to use when he indeed had the running of a war on his hands. Now, as later, he tackled details that other people had not thought worth mentioning.

'It is necessary to state soberly and solemnly that the administration of the military post office during the war in South Africa has not been good. Letters have usually been delayed; many have been sent to the wrong destinations; a considerable proportion has been lost...

'The German army, in which these things are studied, was distinguished during the Franco-Prussian war for the excellence of its postal arrangements in the field. On the Indian Frontier, in victory or defeat, letters and newspapers arrive with strict punctuality. But here in South Africa delay and confusion culminate in hopeless irretrievable loss which has caused, and is causing, intense annoyance and distress throughout the army, and perhaps some dissatisfaction at home.'[13]

But not all was castigation. Characteristically, he found time to relish the lighter moments.

'During the first day at Spion Kop General Hart discovered a soldier sitting safely behind a rock and a long way behind the firing line.
' "Good afternoon, my man," he said in his most nervous, apologetic voice, "what are you doing here?"
' "Sir," replied the soldier, "an officer told me to stop here, sir,"
' "Oh! Why?"
' "I'm a third-class shot, sir."
' "Dear me," said the general after some reflection, "that's an awful pity, because you see you'll have to get quite close to the Boers to do any good. Come along with me and I'll find you a nice place," and a mournful procession trailed off towards the most advanced skirmishers.'[14]

Even at the height of an action, Churchill was inclined to cast aside the mantle of correspondent and assume that of officer, usually of very senior rank. There is, for instance, a delicious eye-witness

account of his haranguing General Sir Charles Warren at the height
of the battle of Spion Kop. He was gesturing widely and through the
continuous gunfire could be heard isolated but passionate phrases
such as 'Remember Majuba' and 'the great British public'. And a
masterly miniature appeared in a regimental paper of the time.

> 'On the stricken field
> See:- With wallets
> Stuffed with ointments
> Balm'd 1st field dressings –
> ever accompanied by his
> faithful Vulture – gently
> chiding erring generals,
> heartening disheartened
> Brigade Majors – the
> prematurely bent figure
> of the late Candidate for
> Oldham, the one lodestone
> of hope to the weary
> soldier.'[15]

Churchill saw a great deal of fighting, observing or taking part in
the major actions of Spion Kop, Dewetsdorp, Vaal Krantz, Pieters,
Johannesburg and Pretoria. He was a member of the first party to
enter Ladysmith and, with his cousin the Duke of Marlborough, was
the first into Pretoria itself, where he 'liberated' the very prison in
which he had been held the year before. The war was therefore a
considerable education to him, as well as a stepping-stone of
unexpected dimensions. In military terms – and indeed in political
and ethical terms also – he was considerably moved. Omdurman,
for all its slaughter, had never been like this. So, in the midst of a
swamp of jingoistic journalism, Churchill stood almost alone in
writing factually, bitterly and honestly. 'I have not been afraid to
write the truth as I see it,' he wrote.

Neither his objectivity regarding the Boers' fighting prowess and
the justice of their cause, nor his respect for them as individuals,
nor his criticism of British administration, strategy and tactics
endeared him to many readers at home, though to an extent his new
reputation obscured by its brilliance what he was actually saying.
But those accustomed to seek out nuance saw all too clearly and,
as in his preceding campaigns, he made bitter enemies. On Sir John
French's return to South Africa, when Churchill had joined Ian

Hamilton's flying column, French initially refused to recognize his existence, and rumours began to circulate that he had broken his parole in escaping — in those days a very damaging accusation. In later years he had to fight more than one libel action before this ghost was finally laid.

In spite of his attacks on the Establishment, Churchill came out of the Boer War with a glittering aura, recognized by his literary peers as a writer of the first importance, and by his political colleagues of the future as a force to be reckoned with. For the despatches that Oliver Borthwick secured at such a high price were worth every penny, comparable to those from the Crimea by William Howard Russell. If his description of Omdurman was an isolated dazzling peak, his dozens of letters from South Africa are a towering chain of mountains dominating everything around. Time and again one meets descriptions of the greatest power and vividness, full of immediacy and yet written with control and awareness. The following, for example, describes one of the many fruitless attacks at Spion Kop.

'But if the attack was superb, the defence was magnificent; nor could the devoted heroism of the Irish soldiers surpass the stout endurance of the Dutch. The artillery redoubled their efforts. The whole summit of the hill was alive with shell. Shrapnel flashed into being above the crests, and the ground sprang up into dust whipped by the showers of bullets and splinters. Again and again whole sections of the entrenchments vanished in an awful uprush of black earth and smoke, smothering the fierce blaze of the lyddite shells from the howitzers and heavy artillery. The cannonade grew to a tremendous thundering hum. Not less than sixty guns were firing continuously on the Boer trenches. But the musketry was never subdued for an instant. Amid the smoke and the dust the slouch hats could still be seen. The Dutch, firm and undaunted, stood to their parapets and plied their rifles with deadly effect.

'The terrible power of the Mauser rifle was displayed. As the charging companies met the storm of bullets they were swept away. Officers and men fell by scores on the narrow ridge. Though assailed in front and flank by the hideous whispering Death, the survivors hurried obstinately onwards, until their own artillery were forced to cease firing, and it seemed, in spite of the bullets, flesh and blood would prevail. But at the last supreme moment the weakness of the attack was shown. The Inniskillings had almost reached their goal. But there were too few to effect their purpose; and when the Boers saw that the attack had withered they shot all the straighter, and several of their boldest leapt out from their trenches and, running forward to meet the soldiers, discharged their magazines at the closest range. It was a frantic scene of blood and fury.'[16]

But Churchill also had an eye for the small things: the unexpected laughter in a lull, a letter clutched in a dead Boer's hand, the strange ambivalence of the fighting man.

'On the way I passed through Sir Charles Warren's camp, and there I found a gang of prisoners...

' "Only forty-eight, sir," said a private soldier, who was guarding them, "and there wouldn't have been so many as that if the officers hadn't stopped us from giving them the bayonet. I never saw such cowards in my life; shoot at you till you come up to them and then beg for mercy. I'd teach 'em." With which remark he turned to the prisoners, who had just been issued rations of beef and biscuit, but who were also very thirsty, and began giving them water from his own canteen, and so left me wondering at the opposite and contradictory sides of human nature as shown by Briton as well as Boer.'[17]

Unlike his two previous books, which had been largely rewritten from the original despatches, the two Boer War books were printed more or less exactly from the newspaper texts. Minor revisions were made and, in *Ian Hamilton's March,* Churchill added extracts from the prison diary of Lieutenant T.H.C. Frankland, who had been captured with him.

In sending the manuscript to his mother, Churchill instructed her to secure an advance of £2000; whether she succeeded or not is unclear, but the following letter to his brother, written during his voyage home from Cape Town, would seem to indicate that she did not.

'My book *London to Ladysmith* had sold when I left Cape Town [4 July] 11,000 copies exclusive of American sales and as it is still going well, it should bring me in a good return. 11,000 means £720 to me.'[18]

The exaggeration of sales figures is a common enough vanity among authors and is usually only a harmless way to boost the ego. In point of fact, the first British edition consisted of only 10,000 copies, published on 15 May, 1900, and followed by a reprint of 500 a few days later. The American edition, which appeared on 16 June, consisted of 3000 copies. The publisher's ledgers do not indicate any further reprints and Churchill was actually being over-sanguine about continuing sales. Nevertheless, he was able to write thirty years later, in *My Early Life,* 'The Sales of *The River War* and of my two books of correspondence from South Africa, together with the ten months' salary amounting to £2500 from the *Morning Post,* had left me in possession of more then £4000.'[19]

In the course of the same letter to his brother, Churchill mentioned that he was working on the sequel, *Ian Hamilton's March.* Five thousand copies of this title appeared on 12 October, 1900, and the strange total of 1533 (presumably 1500 plus 'overs') was published in America on 1 December.

The cost of proof correction was never a problem to daunt Churchill, and both of the Boer War volumes were heavily revised at that stage. In each case extra proofs had to be prepared for him, and in the second volume the charge for correction was more than the original typesetting costs.

Although some personal experiences in the First World War subsequently appeared in print, the publication of *Ian Hamilton's March* marked the end of Churchill's career as war correspondent. Almost simultaneously, and by coincidence, an era was about to end with the death of Queen Victoria. The coincidence was apt, for the war despatches were very much of their time. Churchill wrote of the Queen, the Empire, the Flag with warmth and sincerity, in language that today smacks sometimes of *Boy's Own Paper*; yet he did not write jingoistically. His sentiments were imbued with humanity and charity, and he displayed that chivalric respect − admiration even − for a good enemy, the last flames of which flickered out in the Battle of Britain.

Reminded of the death of Field-Cornet de Mentz in the action at Acton Homes, he wrote:

'De Mentz! The name recalled a vivid scene − the old field-cornet lying forward, grey and grim, in a pool of blood and a litter of empty cartridge cases, with his wife's letter clasped firmly in his stiffening fingers. He had "gone down fighting", and had had no doubts what course to steer. I knew when I saw his face that he had thought the whole thing out....He himself was killed with the responsibility on his shoulders of leading his men into an ambush which, with ordinary precautions, might have been avoided. Such are war's revenges. His widow, a very poor woman, lived next door to the hotel, nursing her son who had been shot through the lungs during the same action. Let us hope he will recover, for he had a gallant sire.'[20]

Churchill has often been accused of glorifying war. He did not;

he relished the excitement of war as a personal experience, as something to set the adrenalin flowing; but few saw more clearly the futility of war, particularly at Omdurman and subsequently when mechanical warfare had succeeded the cleanness of sabre and lance. He tended, admittedly, to view the tragedy less in terms of the loss of life in general than in terms of this or that gallant protagonist. The attitude is almost Arthurian, for surely Churchill was, in spite of Dresden, one of the last survivors of the chivalric age ('In victory – magnanimity'). He mourned the fact of death, but if that death was honourable, or in an honourable cause, he could also celebrate that death. When Lord Ava was fatally wounded he could write, in language that is probably aversive to many of us today, 'Lord Ava is seriously wounded, a sad item, for which the only consolation is that the Empire is worth the blood of its noblest citizens.'[21]

But let it be remembered that, in the same period, and with equal sincerity, he could state: 'War, disguise it as you may, is but a dirty, shoddy business, which only a fool would play at.'

To those caught up by the myth, and particularly those regarding it from an extremist viewpoint, Churchill will probably always remain a warmonger and glorifier of war. To those who take the trouble to read his words as he wrote them, the portrait is at once more complex and more understandable. His war despatches and the related books must be considered in the context of Victorian ethics, politics, social attitudes and, indeed, language. The period was notable for its expansionist campaigns, and it is no coincidence that this period also fathered three of the greatest war correspondents in the history of English language journalism. In the triumvirate of Russell, Steevens and Churchill, it is Churchill who has the strongest claim to be considered *primus inter pares,* even if, as Russell did, he did not bring down a government. Some may well reject the claim, but there can be no denying that his war despatches, written during this limited early period of his life, rank among his finest writings.

His qualities are admirably summed up, with singular appropriateness, by that other eminent war correspondent, G. Ward Price.

'His chief asset as a journalist was an extraordinarily wide field of vision, which enabled him to take in the whole background of a complicated situation. With this was allied a memory of unfailing retentiveness, and a gift for rapid and vivid expression. Supreme self-confidence and complete lack of sensitiveness to opposition or hostility were also valuable factors in the highest class of intellect that has ever put itself at the disposition of the daily Press. Future historians will look to Churchill's despatches to the *Daily Telegraph* and the *Morning Post* for the most reliable and well-balanced records of the campaigns in which he served in the role of war correspondent.'[22]

In 1974, when the collected despatches first appeared in book form,[23] Lord Chalfont reviewed them in similarly enthusiastic terms.

'Although this is, of course, collected journalism which one might normally expect to be completely ephemeral, they do make absorbing reading and in my view the whole thing stands up as a quite distinguished piece of literature....Churchill's despatches are vivid. They're tightly written descriptions of the battlefield in all its colour and in all its horror....There is an amazing quality about his writing, and I don't think anyone reading them could fail to discern the first glimmerings of the massive talent that eventually gave us *Marlborough* and, of course, the history of the Second World War.'[24]

In 1895 Churchill had embarked on a journalistic career with the calculated intention that it should assist him to a parliamentary seat. The deliberate use of authorship as a political weapon proved its efficacy almost immediately, and he continued that use of his literary powers throughout his long life.

By 1900 his writings had secured him his parliamentary career, and in so doing had, almost incidentally, set him on the path that would eventually lead to a Nobel Prize for Literature.

IV

SAVROLA

SAVROLA was Churchill's first book, in the sense that it was well started before the Malakand campaign got under way. An early mention of it comes in a letter to his mother dated 24 August, 1897: 'As to the Novel. I think you will be surprised when you get the MS. It is far and away the best thing I have ever done. I have only written 80 MS pages, but I find a fertility of ideas that surprises me. Whether I publish under my own name or an assumed one — depends on the finished result & ultimately on your opinion. It is called "Affairs of State", a political romance. Scene Plot a hypothetical Republic. Plot briefly what I had sketched to you...but with all sorts of refinements. I am quite enthusiastic about it. All my philosophy is put into the mouth of the hero. But you must see for yourself. It is full of adventure.'

Two days earlier, however, Sir Bindon Blood had summoned Churchill north, and five days after that proud letter to his mother, he had to write: 'The novel is indefinitely shelved. Five chapters are already completed and I am very much pleased with them.'[1]

Nevertheless, even in the middle of military operations, work of a sort went on. 'The novel takes a great deal of shape in my brain. It will I hope be a really good thing. It is certainly original.'[2]

For the next few months Churchill concentrated on *The Story of the Malakand Field Force,* anxious to achieve priority of publication over such rivals as *The Times* correspondent, Lord Fincastle. A little work was done on *Savrola,* however, as a letter dated 10 November shows.

'It had been a great wrench shelving the novel wh had reached its 11th chapter and was progressing capitally, but I realised that this other should be published at once.'

56

Once *Malakand* was out of the way, he returned eagerly to *Savrola*, asking his mother for help on 17 November: '....you must help me with the woman in the novel. She is my chief difficulty. I will bring both these books out before I come home and then we will see whether I may not perhaps supplement my income by writing.' Like all authors —and particularly young ones — his feelings towards his draft flickered occasionally. On 2 December he was writing to his mother again in very cautious and qualifying tones: 'The novel is at present illegible and shelved. I will have it typewritten as soon as possible and send it to you — in part — for your opinion. But you must remember it is in the rough and must be expanded.'

At the end of January, 1898, it was still shelved and Churchill was reading rather than writing: 'The balance between Imports & Exports must be maintained.' In February it was moving again and he was happier. 'The novel is forging slowly along; and I like it better every day. It is destitute of two elements which are rather popular in modern fiction — *squalor and animal emotions* — but for all that I have hopes that it may be attended with some success.'[3]

By March the first draft was almost complete ('though I intend to polish it till it glitters') and work went on for most of 1898, continually laid aside for other, more pressing, events. But by November it was completed and sent home. The Duchess of Marlborough's comments demonstrate a nice mixture of encouragement and cold water.

> 'You have set me a difficult task in the question you ask me to answer! There is so much that is clever and graphic in your Novel and you describe very well, the fighting and the horrors of the Barricades. At the same time there is a want of interest in the plot and I quite agree with you that Lucile is a weak and uninteresting personality. It is clear you have not yet attained a knowledge of Women — and it is evident that you have (I am thankful to see) no experience of Love! Now as to the policy of publishing the Book I can see no objection to it. It cannot injure your reputation in a Literary Point of View for the faults are those of youth and inexperience and not Want of Ability. 250£ is not to be despised and to my mind you have earned it.'[4]

It is impossible to disagree with the Duchess's criticisms, and doubtless Churchill himself accepted them. But there was no time for further revision, for serial rights were snapped up by *Macmillan's Magazine* within a few days. On 29 December he wrote to his mother: 'Please accept Macmillan's offer of £100 for the serial rights of the novel.' But he followed that instruction with an ominous passage, clearly triggered off by Lady Randolph's financial problems, which, as ever, were pressing. 'I fear very much for the future. It is appalling. In three years I can't think what will happen. God only knows, I detest business even more than you do. Years of trouble and squalor are before us. Poverty produced by thoughtlessness will rot your life of peace & happiness, mine of success. These little driblets I make by my pen only make one realise more bitterly.'[5]

A few days later he was again using her as his unpaid agent. 'Macmillan's is alright. Please send any proofs that I can possibly correct in time to me here [Bangalore]. I will return them forthwith. There is a copy in carbon typing of the MS & this I corrected myself roughly. Please see that the publishers get this copy & not the original they have been looking at. I told Jack to give it to Ivor Guest. But he will have finished with it by now. It is the one I sent to the Duchess. This is important. It is a great compliment it's being serialised. Very good and only the successful novels are serialised.'[6]

For all his relative literary inexperience, Churchill was by no means ignorant of the verities of publishing. In a letter dated 26 March, 1899, he wrote to the Duchess of Marlborough: 'The story is to begin publication next month & will run for six months — after which it becomes again my property, and I shall make Longmans publish it in book form in the Autumn. This serial publication is vy satisfactory from a financial point of view as it means an extra hundred pounds — for the value of a book is rather enhanced than depreciated by it.'

Serialization actually started in May, 1899, and continued until September. During this period Longmans agreed to publish in book form and had the type set in America. Two sets of electroplates were made, one being retained for the American edition, and the other shipped to Aberdeen University Press for the British and Colonial editions.

The American edition, consisting of 4000 copies, appeared on 3 February, 1900, followed after ten days by the British edition of 1500 copies for domestic consumption and a similar amount for the Colonial edition. Sales in Britain were remarkably good for a first novel, as the book reprinted twice in the month of publication with further quantities of 2500 and 1000, plus 3000 for the colonies.

After this the novel sank into oblivion until after the Second World War, when it enjoyed an even bigger success with republication in hardback form, several paperback editions and translations into French, German, Finnish, Norwegian, Dutch, Danish, Italian and Spanish.

Churchill's attitude to it after publication was unambiguous. In spite of the fact that up to 1930 it had earned him over £700, he wrote in *My Early Life* that 'I have consistently urged my friends to abstain from reading it'. In 1956, when a new hardback edition appeared in America, he wrote in the foreword that 'the intervening fifty-five years have somewhat dulled though certainly not changed' his opinion of the book.

Initial reactions were mixed. One critic stated that it had 'literary merit of high order,' which must be considered an exaggeration; and several compared Churchill to Disraeli − an ironic echo of the sarcastic description of *The Story of the Malakand Field Force* ('A volume by Disraeli revised by a mad printer's reader'). While reviewers seemed more or less unanimous in their praise of the action scenes ('brilliant in the extreme,' wrote one), they were equally unanimous about the weak characterization. The critic of *The Echo* called the plot 'singularly light and not too well elaborated. Add to this that his love scenes are shirked as far as possible, that his heroine, unlike his men, is little more than a lay figure and that his dialogue makes too desperate efforts after intellectuality (and therefore dullness) and you will see that Mr Winston Churchill scarcely possesses at present all the qualifications of a successful romancer. Still, as a talented young author's first attempt in an unfamiliar vein, *Savrola* merits being regarded as a novel of undoubted interest and no little promise.'

The *Star* took a similar line, though its reviewer saw more virtue than his colleague on the *Echo*. 'It will not add to the reputation he gained by *The River War*, compared with which it is in many respects crude and immature; but it is, nevertheless, a brilliant, witty and exciting political tale.' The critic goes on to display a striking perspicuity in a further − and less flattering − comparison with Disraeli.

> 'Mr. Churchill follows the Disraelian tradition. He is ambitious; he is a perfect poseur; and he is an adept in the arts of notoriety. He has turned war correspondence into a gigantic advertisement of his modest personality. The novel is a sideshow which, as Dizzy knew, is an excellent means of keeping up public interest.'

Churchill was not to use the novel form again; he had more direct methods and more important themes to lay before the public. But we have already seen, in his approach to his campaign books, how calculated was his use of the printed word to further his political ambitions. And in the case of *Savrola* too the calculation was strong. The novel is at once a political testament and a writing-out of a stage of personal development. Michael Wolff, in his study of Churchill, observed that 'those of a psychological bent may profess to see in Churchill's casting of his mother as Lucile and his father as her husband, Molara, the expression of an Oedipus complex, or at least of a Hamlet-Gertrude-Claudius syndrome.' Mr Wolff, I think, misses the point by casting Lord Randolph as Molara, for the matter is not that simple. Certainly Lady Randolph was largely the model for Lucile, though there is evidence that her character was sketched for Churchill at his request by his aunt Leonie. Churchill had had little experience of women at this point in his life (as his grandmother had so tartly observed), and some of Lucile is clearly his mother. But only some, for not even the immature and inexperienced son could have created such a shallow character from the sole inspiration of Lady Randolph. Whatever faults she had, she was by no means vapid and uninteresting, nor was she quite so politically and emotionally negative as Lucile, who clearly had rarely suffered from anything remotely resembling a thought-process until she met Savrola.

Savrola and Molara, however, are a different matter, for (*pace* Mr Wolff) they represent different aspects of Lord Randolph and his son; two fictional characters together portraying two factual people. At this early stage in his political development, as might be expected, the son's stance was largely a reflection of the father's; and, in spite of Churchill's statement that 'all my philosophy is put into the mouth of the hero', the ideologies and functions of the two characters remain intertwined. To Molara he gave Lord Randolph's right-wing authoritarianism, his dogmatism, his proclivity for treachery and, Churchill's endeavours to the contrary notwithstanding, his undeniable charisma. To Savrola he gave his idealistic (and probably impracticable) political vision and sense of the future; a paternalistic and democratic concern for 'the people.'

Further, there is a certain ambivalence in Churchill's attitude to Molara, as there was towards his father. Even though he is portraying a cruel, tyrannical dictator, given over to force and violence, he cannot prevent attractive − or at least admirable − traits from appearing in the character. Molara possesses a single-mindedness, a dynamic force that his creator clearly respects and at times almost envies. One can see the authoritarian in Churchill emerging from time to time, in spite of his intended allegiance to the revolutionary creed of Savrola. Indeed, Molara is in many ways a far more positive figure than the hero.

There is in Savrola little, if any, evidence of a sense of humour, for instance; indeed he is, it must be admitted, a bit of a prig. With his sights set immovably on achieving power in Laurania, his ethics firmly entrenched, he is capable of expounding a creed which, though doubtless a model of rectitude, has a chilling effect in its superiority and pomposity.

'Would you rise in the world? You must work while others amuse themselves. Are you desirous of a reputation for courage? You must risk your life. Would you be strong morally and physically? You must resist temptation. All this is paying in advance; that is prospective finance. Observe the other side of the picture; the bad things are paid for afterwards.'

Is it being too fanciful to imagine that the last phrase is an oblique comment on his father's fate?

Savrola, for all his revolutionary attitudes, has only a partial control of events; and this again is a characteristic of Lord Randolph. One wonders, in fact, whether Savrola, once in power, could actually have ruled a country — as, indeed, one must wonder about Lord Randolph. There is little personal force in Savrola, for all that Churchill doggedly describes it.

But if the characters are pasteboard, what of the plot? In itself it is simple — the story of a coup to unseat Molara, President of Laurania. The uprising succeeds insofar as Molara is deposed and killed, though the ending of the story is left open, with the revolutionary forces being stood off by a loyal gunboat in the harbour, and Savrola fleeing into exile with Lucile. The events themselves, the moves and counter-moves, the attacks and counter-attacks — indeed, the purely military derring-do bits — are well and often vividly handled. But the main hypothesis crumbles on examination, for would the totalitarian Molara, knowing Savrola's intentions as he does, have tolerated his continued existence, let alone his agitational meetings and plottings? Perhaps at the turn of the century dictators were different, though it does not seem likely, and history argues otherwise. The social context which Churchill wraps round the political confrontation immediately invalidates the basic concept of the novel, for the unwritten rules of the officers' mess and the cricket pavilion seem to regulate revolutionary behaviour to an unbelievable degree; reigning President and subversive enemy meet and gently chide each other at formal balls. Savrola would, in reality, have met the firing squad long before the novel opens.

And yet, and yet. It is perhaps unfair to be too harsh about *Savrola*, not because it is written by Churchill and therefore in some strange way sacrosanct, but because it is a beginner's work of undeniable interest and vivacity, because it exemplifies the young man's political philosophy (and possibly in ways he did not altogether intend), and because it contains felicities with which many a more mature writer would have been pleased. What happens when civilisation degenerates? A young officer coins the epigram: 'Our morals will be gone, but our Maxims will remain.' The young would-be politician defines civilization: 'A state of society where moral force begins to escape from the tyranny of physical forces.'

Nevertheless, *Savrola* is a failure taken as a whole. Its main interest is now extrinsic. Written in the mould of the 'rattling good yarn' of such contemporary writers as William le Queux or the early Sapper and Oppenheim, it fails to rise to their standard, not even possessing the wealth of unintentional funniness present in le Queux. The fact that all except two of its many reprints appeared after 1945 is proof enough that its revival was not due to literary considerations. It remains Churchill's only novel (and with the exception of three short stories his only attempt at fiction); as such it occupies a minor but intriguing place in the canon. Churchill would never have made a novelist and he surely realized this. In any case, the opportunity did not arise again, for henceforward his writing was about harsh reality, and the result of experience rather than imagination.

V

THE SPEECHES

IT is perhaps surprising that, during his long lifetime of politics and authorship, Churchill never wrote anything remotely resembling a work of political theory; or, indeed, barring some relatively lightweight journalistic efforts, any work concerning political practice. It can, in fact, be said that he *wrote* no specifically political book at all, for all the titles concerned with either domestic or foreign political subjects are collections of speeches (with the exception of *Step by Step,* which is a collection of newspaper articles from the *Daily Telegraph* and London *Evening Standard*). Politics in a general sense obtrudes into *Thoughts and Adventures,* while the majority of the portraits in *Great Contemporaries* are of politicians; but for the most part his political testament in book form rests in his printed speeches.

Disraeli, as has been noted, used his novels as a means of keeping himself before the public eye. Churchill's methods were more direct. Like Disraeli, he continued the debate between the covers of a book, but the books were precisely related to whatever he was involved in at the time. From his first slim volume of speeches on army reform to the five rather anticlimactic volumes of postwar speeches, he carried his campaigns to the fireside with relentless continuity.

Churchill is often described as the last of the great masters of rhetoric, a quality that owes its existence to the fact that he began his career in the last days of the Victorian era and enjoyed his early period of success in Edwardian times. Politicians nowadays do not indulge in rhetoric — a suspect device at the best of times, and one doubly suspicious in these hard-eyed days. Indeed, politicians have gone far the other way, and the lingering phrases of the past three decades seem to have centred themselves around the use of slang. (This was, of course, a trick that Churchill by no means scorned;

but he used it as a contrast, a deliberate anticlimax for effect, not as a disingenuous attempt to 'talk to the people'.)[1]

His experience in the leisurely Victorian and Edwardian parliaments, the example of his father and the strong influence of an early friend, the American politician Bourke Cockran,[2] combined with the strengths and weaknesses of his literary models, laid the foundation of his style. And accustomed as he was to public speaking, it is no surprise that from an early date he dictated rather than wrote his books.[3]

The interlinking and interaction of Churchill's written and spoken styles can be considered at once a virtue and a vice. Too often he was seduced by the fine, the rolling phrase; too often, particularly in moments when facts were more important than emotions, he permitted himself indulgences that a lesser stylist would not have dared. Doubtless such passages are to be expected in speeches, but they present dangers in the written word. The British tend to distrust the more ornate stylists; to play with words, to intoxicate one's self with phrases, is considered more characteristic of Italian, French or Irish literature than of our own. A style that is too overtly considered can bring out the critical hatchets.

Churchill's spoken style changed, it must be admitted, over the years. As a young man he proved himself adept at mastering masses of figures and facts, and he learned to use them coherently and effectively. Considering the early speeches from the distance of up to ninety years, one must necessarily be grateful for this skill in presenting a case. Even his maiden speech, written out weeks beforehand and laboriously memorized, is impressively lucid and logical. In later years he relied on notes which, in their layout, frequently resembled 'modern' verse, especially that of William Carlos Williams.[4]

Almost without exception, however, the subjects which engrossed Churchill in his early days as a politician are now long-forgotten, and the main interest those speeches still have, therefore, is to provide a guide to his thoughts at the time, and an indication of stylistic and political development.

Between 1903 and 1961 Churchill published no fewer than eighteen volumes of speeches. In addition to these, there were scores of pamphlets and several selections and collections. It is perhaps arguable that such publications should not be considered in an assessment of Churchill as a writer, since many speeches were extempore, and none was initially intended for print. But to adopt such an attitude would be narrow indeed; his publications were weapons in a series of campaigns and, after all, books are books whatever method of composition is used. And if Churchill, far more than any other politician of his day, regarded his speeches as worth recording, then it would be blatantly unbalanced to ignore them.

Initially two factors prompted Churchill to print his speeches from an early point in his political career. In the first place there was no other way to communicate his actual words to the public. Newspaper reports were inevitably edited and often written in paraphrase form. Even his parliamentary speeches were not initially printed in full, since *Hansard* did not publish verbatim texts until 1911.

Secondly, he knew only too well the impermanence of the merely spoken word; in a significant passage in *Savrola* he had written: 'He...knew nothing good could be obtained without effort. These impromptu feats of oratory existed only in the minds of the listeners; the flowers of rhetoric were hothouse plants.'

From early days, therefore, Churchill preserved his hothouse plants like a nineteenth-century maiden — by pressing them between the covers of a book.

His first major speech in the House of Commons concerned Army Reform, the very subject that had finally toppled his father, and it is therefore singularly fitting that his first volume of speeches should be on the same topic. The Secretary of State for War was then St John Brodrick[5] who, in the aftermath of the Boer War, was demanding increased expenditure on the army; not only that, he was making organizational proposals that Churchill considered extremely unsound. He attacked Brodrick relentlessly both in the House and outside, and in 1903 published an extended pamphlet entitled *Mr Brodrick's Army*.

Two extracts will suffice to demonstrate not only the young politician's hard hitting, but also his sheer impishness in making his points, the precocious duellist teasing his lumbering opponent.

'...I have not the slightest hesitation in telling you — indeed, I think it is my duty to tell you, indeed, I should be cowardly and dishonest, if knowing what I do, and feeling as I do, on this question, I were to conceal the truth from you, and to join the great conspiracy in keeping the public in the dark — now, after two years, I have no hesitation in saying that Mr Brodrick's scheme of 1901 is a total, costly, ghastly failure. There has been a great increase of expenditure without any proportionate increase of efficiency. Wonderful reforms have been carried out — on paper. Some things have been turned upside down and others have been turned inside out, old things have been called by new names and new combinations have been made of the same old things. Within the space of two years the Secretary of State for War has put forward a perfect series of conflicting and often contradictory proposals. Two years ago he told the country that no increase of the soldier's pay was necessary; last year he came to Parliament and asked for an increase of the soldier's pay. Two years ago he told us that he adhered to a system of enlistment whereby men serve seven years in the Army and five with the Reserve, and last year he came down to the House of Commons with a new plan of their serving three years with the colours and nine with the Reserve, and only last autumn, such is his confusion of mind – I am sorry to speak so plainly, particularly at what may be an unseasonable moment – he introduced into the House of Commons a Bill called the Militia and Yeomanry Bill, one part of which proposed to make a reserve for the Militia out of men who had served in the Regular Army, and the other part of which proposed to make a reserve for the Regular Army out of men who had served in the Yeomanry. That is a plan which rather reminds one of people who are said to make a living by taking in each other's washing.'[6]

And again:

'The Fourth Army Corps has just got its commander, Lord Grenfell, and he was so glad at getting this appointment that at Malta the other day he received Mr Brodrick, whom he no doubt mistook for the Commander-in-Chief, with a salute of fifteen cannons at the public expense. But while the Fourth Army Corps has got its general, the general has not yet got his army corps, though I observe from the papers that he is to take up command on the 1st of April. As for the two remaining army corps, they are still in the air, organised, apparently, on the Marconi system....Nearly four months ago you might have read in the newspapers an official *communiqué* from the War Office to this effect – "General Bruce Hamilton is appointed to command the Third Division of the First Army Corps."...But what the public do not see – unless it is pointed out to them by inconvenient and tiresome people like me – is that this same general has no division to command at all, because there is no Third Division of the First Army Corps yet formed. Nor is there likely to be for a long time to come...[The general's] name is being exploited for a purely political purpose, namely, to make believe that Mr Brodrick's scheme is much further advanced than it really is or is likely to be.'[7]

Little is known of the publishing history of *Mr Brodrick's Army*. Bearing the imprint of Arthur L. Humphreys,[8] its first form was a small forty-four-page leaflet of undistinguished appearance and a high level of illegibility. Closely-packed and minute type deters all but the most dogged and hawk-eyed reader, and it seems clear that Churchill rejected this first attempt on the part of Humphreys and demanded a new, larger and more substantial production. Only one copy of this first version is known, which is contained in the Churchill Archives.

Shortly afterwards it re-appeared in a more spacious quarto format with red card wrappers. Even in this guise it is probably the rarest of all Churchill editions, together with its sister-publication *For Free Trade*. It cannot now be ascertained how many copies were printed, or how many sold. But from the fact that it was still being advertised on the wrapper of *For Free Trade* some three years later it can be inferred that it was not a best-seller.

The same can be said of its companion, which appeared in April, 1906, again under the imprint of Arthur L. Humphreys. Both topics were of major − even vital − importance, in their day, but both in time receded in importance, and neither book has been reprinted except in the Centenary Collected Edition.[9]

Liberalism and the Social Problem (1909) and *The People's Rights* (1910) are of rather greater significance, if only because they evoke Churchill's radical phase, during which he was responsible for legislation which was, for its day, positively socialist: The Shop Hours Act, The Mines Eight Hours Bill, the creation of labour exchanges and unemployment insurance. These were policies which clearly owned more than a little to the brooding spirit of Lord Randolph, reflecting some of his idealistic political paternalism in both the theory and the practice they illustrate. Perhaps less to Lord Randolph's taste were his son's savage attacks on the House of Lords; in the latter book he demanded 'the settlement for ever of the evil, ugly veto of the Peers, which they have used so ill so long'. And not only was the veto under siege, but also the much wider question of the Peers' intrinsic attitudes.

'I feel myself offended by the air of autocratic insolence in which the House of Lords indulge. Lord Curzon quotes a great French agnostic and adopts his phrase. "All civilisations are the work of aristocracies". It would be much more true to say that the upkeep of aristocracies has been the hard work of civilisations....What does Lord Lansdowne say about old-age pensions? He says, "We allowed them to pass". More than that, he said in a recent speech at Plymouth, "We have allowed a lot of bills to pass − the Port of London, Labour Exchanges, Small Holdings, the

Patents Bill." We have allowed a lot of them to pass! We have given you a lot of rope, you miserable members of the House of Commons! Why, we have never thrown out a Budget before this year; we have allowed all this, and yet you complain, yet you unreasonable Radicals are not satisfied with all our generosity, all our magnanimity! That is their point of view. Very often a man shows much more his real inner point of view in a single unguarded phrase which slips out straight from the mint of his mind than he does in the most carefully prepared diplomatic statement or most eloquent peroration.

'What does it mean − "We have allowed them to pass"? It means that the hereditary institution which Lord Lansdowne leads regards all our liberties and political rights as enjoyed and enjoyable only so long as they choose to let us go on having them. But once we touch reality, once we touch their interests and privileges − "Out!" '[10]

Unsurprisingly, he was equally scathing about Tariff Reform.

'Everything depends upon the issue of this election. Lies are told you. The party of property and monopoly, the party of privilege and class interest were afraid of the cruel sufferings of poverty, for they invented a lie to palliate the claims of the suffering. That lie is Protection. It was invented in order to give the propertied classes the means of warding off the insistent claims for social and remedial legislation for the masses of the population in our great cities. It was invented to give them something to answer. Those who pointed to the miserable conditions of large masses of our communities have been given their answer, but it is a dodge, a cheat, and there is not one word of honesty about it. I am convinced that the whole of the Tariff Reform movement is an interested attempt by the privileged classes in order to secure them all they enjoy at present, and to carry their warfare, their inroads, further upon the rights and interests of the common people.'[11]

Even allowing for election fever, this is a quite remarkable passage. Any blindfold test would surely indicate some fiery Marxist like H.M. Hyndman as speaker rather than Churchill, who was, if anyone was, a member of the privileged class himself. It is, in its language and attitude, positively communistic; indeed, to be honest, it smacks of nothing so much as a street-corner harangue by one of P.G. Wodehouse's hairy socialists in its cliché-ridden fervour. But it is symptomatic of the radical Churchill, who could fight tooth and nail for a philosophy in terms that he would have abjured a few years before and a few years after. While a commitment lasted, however, it was passionate and absolute, and these were attributes that were of vital importance between 1939 and 1945.

Five thousand copies of *Liberalism and the Social Problem* were published by Hodder and Stoughton in the week ending 26 November, 1909, followed by an American edition from Doubleday Doran on 5 February, 1910. There has been no reprint.

An unknown quantity of *The People's Rights,* in simultaneous hardback and paperback editions, appeared during the week ending 14 January, 1910, also from Hodder and Stoughton. One further edition was published by Jonathan Cape in 1970 with an introduction by Cameron Hazlehurst.

Both remain valuable reminders of a phase in Churchill's life that he describes nowhere else in his writings, only fleetingly in his journalism, and that is all too often forgotten in the public mind.

Twenty years were to pass before another collection of speeches appeared in print. The second decade of the century was largely taken up with preparation for war and war itself, while during the early years of the following decade he was engrossed in *The World Crisis*. But 1931 saw the publication of *India*.

During the late twenties, in spite of holding cabinet rank, Churchill found himself increasingly at loggerheads with the official policy of the Conservative Party and in 1929 entered the wilderness in which he remained for ten years. Much of the reason for the continuing ostracism lay in his unrelenting opposition to Hitler[12] and his equally unrelenting demands for military preparedness; but another, and earlier, reason lay in his bitter opposition to Baldwin's India policy. Increasingly perturbed by developments and philosophies that he regarded as destructive of all that India meant to Britain (which included the proposal to give it dominion status) he attacked Government policy in the House, the halls and the Press. And it was characteristic of his thinking that the epigraph to *India* should come from Disraeli: 'The key to India is London; the majesty of sovereignty, the spirit and vigour of your Parliament, the inexhaustible resources, the ingenuity and determination of your people – *these are the keys of India.*'

Churchill had always hit hard; not for him a round of gentlemanly sparring between friends. His fight to maintain full control of India employed not just the clenched fist but the bludgeon.

'What spectacle could be more sorrowful than that of this powerful country casting away with both hands, and up till now almost by general acquiescence, the great inheritance which centuries have gathered? What spectacle could be more strange, more monstrous in its perversity, than to see the Viceroy and the high officials and agents of the Crown in India labouring with all their influence and authority to unite and weave together into a confederacy all the forces adverse and hostile to our rule in India?... It is a hideous act of self-mutilation, astounding to every nation in the world. The princes, the Europeans, the Moslems, the Depressed classes, the Anglo-Indians – none of them know what to do nor where to turn in the face of their apparent desertion by Great Britain....I am against this surrender to Gandhi. I am against these conversations and agreements between Lord Irwin and Mr Gandhi. Gandhi stands for the expulsion of Britain from India. Gandhi stands for the permanent exclusion of British trade from India. Gandhi stands for the substitution of Brahmin domination for British rule in India. You will never be able to come to terms with Gandhi....In running after Gandhi and trying to build on Gandhi, in imagining that Mr Ramsay MacDonald and Mr Gandhi and Lord Irwin are going to bestow peace and progress on India, we should be committing ourselves to a crazy dream, with a terrible awakening.'[13]

The book was published on 27 May, 1931, by Thornton Butterworth in both hardback and paperback editions. It remains a minor book on a long-since academic subject, but still useful for its powerful summaries of the arguments of the period.

During the Thirties, Churchill worked on his biography of the first Duke of Marlborough and began the first draft of his *History of the English-Speaking Peoples*. At the same time he kept up his unrelenting attacks on Germany. He had warned of the possibility of such a threat in *The World Crisis* and in articles subsequently published in *Thoughts and Adventures* and *Great Contemporaries*. Soon the reality of his prophecies was there for those who wished to see it. In the years immediately preceding the war, he devoted two books to the subject, *Arms and the Covenant* (which, in America, had the more direct title of *While England Slept*) and *Step by Step*.[14]

Five thousand copies of *Arms and the Covenant* were published by Harrap on 24 June, 1938. The idea had come from his son Randolph, and the father acknowledged this by entrusting him with the selection and editing, the first time he had trusted anyone in this way since his disastrous experiences at the hands of his uncle Moreton Frewen, in 1898. The message was spelled out by the brief, stark section titles: Germany disarmed; Germany rearming; Germany rearmed. As a collection of speeches it remains magnificent. Churchill was both cold and passionate as he detailed the threat to Britain and the rest of Europe. Together with *Step by Step*, it is the permanent record of one man's unceasing struggle in the face of resentment, apathy and complacency. In many ways it is more important even than the collections of wartime speeches that were to follow, and is therefore probably the most crucial volume of speeches that he ever published, in which every form of persuasion from invective to sarcasm was used.

'We are now in our third year of openly avowed rearmament. Why is it, if all is going well, there are so many deficiencies? Why, for instance, are the Guards drilling with flags instead of machine guns? Why is it that our small Territorial Army is in a rudimentary condition? Is that all according to schedule? Why should it be, when you consider how small are our forces? Why should it be impossible to equip the Territorial Army simultaneously with the Regular Army? It would have been a paltry task for British industry, which is more flexible and fertile than German industry in every sphere except munitions....If Germany is able to produce in these three years equipment and armament of every kind for its Air Force and for sixty or seventy divisions of the Regular Army, how is it that we have been unable to furnish our humble, modest military forces with what is necessary? If you had given the contract to Selfridge or to the Army and Navy Stores, I believe that you would have had the stuff today.'[15]

At the time of Munich, unrepentant, he continued to stand alone in a House full of self-congratulation.

'Between submission and immediate war there was this third alternative, which gave a hope not only of peace but of justice. It is quite true that such a policy in order to succeed demanded that Britain should declare straight out and a long time beforehand that she would, with others, join to defend Czechoslovakia against an unprovoked aggression. His Majesty's Government refused to give that guarantee when it could have saved the situation, yet in the end they gave it when it was too late, and now, for the future, they renew it when they have not the slightest power to make it good.
'All is over. Silent, mournful, abandoned, broken, Czechoslovakia recedes into the darkness. She has suffered in every respect by her

association with the Western democracies and with the League of Nations, of which she has always been an obedient servant. She has suffered in particular from her association with France, under whose guidance and policy she has been actuated for so long...

'There must always be the most profound regret and sense of vexation in British hearts at the treatment and misfortunes which have overcome the Czechoslovakian Republic. They have not ended here. At any moment there may be a hitch in the programme. At any moment there may be an order for Herr Goebbels to start again his propaganda of calumny and lies; at any moment an incident may be provoked, and now that the fortress line is given away what is there to stop the will of the conqueror?'[16]

Hindsight is strange. How, one wonders from the vantage-point of the present, could the truth of Churchill's warnings *not* be seen? Much is made of this country's habit of muddling through, its amateurism, its perpetual unreadiness; in spite of continuing lack of preparation through the centuries we have somehow survived since 1066, and the string of eventual victories ('damned near-run things') has actually enhanced and hallowed the habit. In the Thirties, surely the last bastion of the archetypal English gentleman, the attitude was too deeply ingrained for even Churchill's searing vision to succeed. (And there were other, darker, less honourable considerations as well. See note 12.)

Three years later he published his first book of wartime speeches, under the title *Into Battle*.[17] It was, in fact, the brainchild of Desmond Flower, then Literary Director of Cassell, who, until then, had published nothing by Churchill,[18] though they had acquired the rights of *A History of the English-Speaking Peoples* a decade earlier. Flower suggested that a volume of speeches would be timely, important and successful, and it was agreed that he himself should undertake the selection and editing. The project was only half-completed when he went into the army, and the task was taken on by Randolph Churchill. He too went into the army, and the job went to Charles Eade, then Editor of the *Sunday Dispatch,* who prepared this and all subsequent volumes of wartime speeches.

As might be expected, the book was highly successful. An initial edition of 30,000 copies appeared in February, 1941, followed by reprints totalling roughly the same amount again. Eventually translations appeared in French, Finnish, Czechoslovakian, Spanish, Swedish, Italian, Danish, Norwegian, Portuguese, German, Hebrew and Hungarian; naturally the majority of these appeared after the war. In America, where it was entitled *Blood, Sweat, and Tears,* over 60,000 copies were quickly sold. And there now also began a five-year period in which copies of individual speeches, excerpts, quotations and exhortations rained down upon occupied Europe and enemy Europe through the combined efforts of the Political Warfare Executive and the Royal Air Force.[19]

Given this excellent start, it was natural for both publisher and Prime Minister to continue the process; and it was good for national morale into the bargain. Thereafter a collection appeared each year of the war and beyond: *The Unrelenting Struggle* (1942, 55,000 sales in the English language and eleven translations); *The End of the Beginning* (1943, 45,500 sales in the English language and nine translations); *Onwards to Victory* (1944, 36,500 sales in English and ten translations); *The Dawn of Liberation* (1945, 37,500 sales in English and nine translations); and finally *Victory* (1946, 43,000 sales in English and eight translations.)

In the autumn of 1946 the process was completed by the publication of the slim volume of *Secret Session Speeches* (almost 60,000 sales).

In 1946 also came the first of many selections; *War Speeches 1940-1945*. Bound simply in white card wrappers, the book sold over 20,000 copies in the United Kingdom alone, while translations of selected speeches (not all identical) appeared in thirteen languages, including Egyptian, Serbian and Russian.

With these speeches, together with *Arms and the Covenant,* we have the clearest possible picture of Churchill the gladiator, the fighter, waging war with words as well as with bombs and bullets. No one knew better than he the propaganda value across the world not only of his constant refusal to admit defeat (though he acknowledged passing set-backs in the House of Commons) but also of his never-tiring assertions of eventual victory. Then, if ever, he used every weapon in his formidable armoury, from high-flown rhetoric to controlled bathos, from irresistible exhortation to simple slander. He bullied, he cajoled, he inspired, weaving a national body-armour from pungent phrases. He himself claimed merely to express what everyone would have said, given the opportunity and the skill: 'It fell to me...to express [the nation's] sentiments on suitable occasions.' And, as always, there was, beneath and within everything he said, his near-mythical view of British — and especially English — history, its varied course a golden thread of duty and leadership throughout the centuries.

'Two Sundays ago all the bells rang to celebrate the victory of our Desert Army at Alamein. Here was a martial episode in British history which deserved a special recognition. But the bells also carried with their clashing joyous peals our thanksgiving that, in spite of all our errors and shortcomings, we have been brought nearer to the frontiers of deliverance. We have not reached those frontiers yet, but we are becoming ever more entitled to be sure that the awful perils which might well have blotted out our life and all that we love and cherish will be surmounted, and that we shall be preserved for further service in the vanguard of mankind.'[20]

And in one of several speeches on 8 May, 1945 (VE Day), he still hammered home his belief in the almost God-given role of leadership and inspiration, both in the past and in years to come.

'My dear friends, this is your hour. This is not a victory of a party or a class. It is a victory of the great British nation as a whole. We were the first, in this ancient island, to draw the sword against tyranny. After a while we were left all alone against the most tremendous military power that has been seen. We were alone for a whole year.

'There we stood, alone. Did anyone want to give in? [Cries of 'No!'] Were we down-hearted? ['No!'] The lights went out and the bombs came down. But every man, woman and child in the country had no thoughts of quitting the struggle. London can take it. So we came back after long months from the jaws of death, out of the mouth of hell, while all the world wondered. When shall the reputation and faith of this generation of English men and women fail? I say that in the long years to come not only will the people of this island but of the world, wherever the bird of freedom chirps in human hearts, look back to what we have done and they will say "Do not despair, do not yield to violence and tyranny, march straight forward and die if need be — unconquered." '[21]

But, characteristically, after the noble sentiments came still the warning, the exhortation: a war was won but new enemies awaited, and Churchill, true to his vision of destiny, tried to make sure that the country understood its continuing role.

'I told you hard things at the beginning of these last five years; you did not shrink, and I should be unworthy of your confidence and generosity if I did not still cry: Forward, unflinching, unswerving, indomitable, till the whole task is done and the whole world is safe and clean.'[22]

74

But, as in the Thirties, the country did not heed.

For Churchill the next few years were largely spent in writing his war memoirs, but he also published a series of five volumes of postwar speeches, all selected and edited by Randolph Churchill. Wartime fervour, however, had quickly faded into postwar reaction and apathy, and few wanted to read the words of the new Leader of the Opposition. *Sinews of Peace* (1948) had a first edition of only 10,000 copies and was not reprinted. *Europe Unite* (1950) went to 12,000 copies of which 2500 were exported to America; again there was no reprint. *In the Balance* (1951) dropped to 8200 copies, of which 2000 went to America. *Stemming the Tide* (1953) dropped still further to 5500, of which America took only 1850. And *The Unwritten Alliance* (1961), Churchill's last book, was printed in a single edition of 5000 copies only.[23]

Much of the decline can, of course, be laid to the fatigue of the aftermath of war. Whatever high zeal there had been when it began soon degenerated into hard slog; and if people had been willing still to be roused by Churchill's oratory during the later stages of the war, few wanted to be reminded of it afterwards. Immediately after the war, Churchill was once more in eclipse; and by the time he returned to lead the country again, he was already tired and ill, a fraction of his former self. His postwar speeches show this only too clearly; in comparison with the vigour of *Arms and the Covenant* and the superb drive of the early war speeches, those of the Fifties are rather sad. The spirit still brooded mightily above the country, but its force had been spent in that last herculean effort. As Lord Moran has shown in his revealing but often regrettable book, the spirit knew this itself, and the country sensed it instinctively.

Then again, the postwar years were not the time for the high-flown Churchillian rhetoric. The people had had enough of exhortations, and had other things on their minds. Churchill, for instance, was already proposing a Common Market (or, more accurately, he had returned to it again for the first time since the Thirties, when it had figured largely in his speeches and writings),[24] but that was altogether too rarified for an exhausted Britain more concerned with recovering from exertion and already losing the will to work that still largely eludes it today.

Part of the anticlimax was, however, built in. Churchill's period of ascendancy was necessarily a highly emotional time, resonant with bugles and alarms. How *could* the fine words sound afterwards? How *could* the sentiments of the Atlantic Charter sound in the nuclear age? Could there not be an altogether too pointed irony? There could and there was. For all their sadness, their aura of lost strength, the postwar speeches offered uncomfortable reading to a disheartened nation. And if this is true of the postwar speeches, it is doubly true of those of the war. Couched in a language that is nowadays strange to us, redolent as it is with echoes of the Edwardian and even the Victorian eras, containing sentiments and ideals now completely and utterly at variance with the driving obsessions of today, Churchill's speeches now present a posthumous goad, an unwanted reminder of past days. His gleaming vision of Britain's destiny lay in ruins, seen as a distorted sepulchre of colonialism, expansionism, class suspicion and arrogance. And what had those qualities to do with the newly-socialised Britain of the Forties and early Fifties?

Nevertheless...

Even now the sonorous phrases sometimes have the power to move, even if it is only though a conjuration of the *sound* of that rumbling voice; and we do not like to be moved any more. To use a once-fashionable phrase, Churchill was not cool. And this judgment is nothing whatsoever to do with the fact that he was a Conservative or even a 'warmonger'; it is simply and basically that he *felt* and was not afraid to express emotions fully and, if need be, nakedly. He wept easily. He was a man of large sympathies and large emotions; and these are aversive characteristics in the Britain of today.

This conclusion, sadly accurate though it is, possibly says more about the audience than the speaker, the reader than the writer. Is it possible yet to come to terms with his speeches, or are events still too crowded round and over us? To an extent it is, though later generations may alter our verdicts, as they so often do. Churchill wrote a lot and said a lot during his long life; it is unrealistic to expect everything to be on a uniformly high plane. The mere passage of time wipes away the effectiveness of much that he said. The early speeches are now of only minor significance. The postwar speeches might appear on the surface to hold more importance because they are closer and several of their topics are still very much with us. *Arms and the Covenant* and the six volumes of wartime speeches still claim the highest level, provided it is clear that not all the individual speeches are of the utmost quality. But, as volumes, they reflect the supreme achievement of Churchill's life and therefore automatically claim equivalent importance. And this is only right, since the events they evoke called forth his mightiest oratorical efforts. (Though in 1953 he denied being an orator. 'An orator,' he said, 'is spontaneous.')

It is sometimes noticeable that, now the voice is silent, even the gramophone records cannot always capture the intensity, the magic, the inspiration of those wartime words. As Hazlitt wrote, 'The orator's vehemence and gesture, the loudness of the voice, the speaking eye, the conscious attitude, the inexplicable dumb show and noise − all those brave sublunary things that made his raptures clear − are no longer there, and without those he is nothing.'

A long way from nothing, surely; but perhaps one had to be there. Not only is the vocal presence essential, but also, political speeches are by their very nature as transient as the fleeting events they once sought to illuminate. One can, appropriately enough, leave the matter to Lord Rosebery, who knew all about these things.

> 'No-one reads old speeches any more than old sermons....The more brilliant and telling they were at the time, the more dolorous the quest. The lights are extinguished; the flowers are faded; the voice seems cracked across the empty space of years, it sounds like a message from a remote telephone; one wonders if that can really be the scene that fascinated and inspired....It all seems as flat as decanted champagne....Genuine political speeches that win the instant laurels of debate soon lose their savour. All the accompaniments have disappeared − the heat, the audience, the interruptions, and the applause; and what remains seems cold and flabby.'[25]

Churchill understood from the very beginning of his political career that mere words are impermanent. He probably understood also, as clearly as his old mentor and friend, the truth about old speeches. Nevertheless, to the end of his parliamentary career, he continued to take the necessary defensive action − as any good fighter should.

VI

JOURNALISM

AS earlier chapters have shown, Churchill laid down the foundations of both his political and his literary careers through his early war correspondence. Having proved its effectiveness as an extra-parliamentary weapon, he maintained his involvement with journalism throughout his life, in the course of which he published over 800 articles, the majority of which were not reprinted in his lifetime.

Although a few pieces appeared during the first decade (both of the century and Churchill's political life) he was then primarily concerned with consolidating his parliamentary position and reputation; and, after 1908, with Cabinet responsibilities. To a limited extent he used the Press for agitational purposes and, during the First World War, for the publication of morale-boosting features on the progress of the Allies' campaigns.[1] But once the war was over he turned more and more to journalism, both as a channel for political argument and as a source of income. In the Thirties, although he wrote *Marlborough* and began the first draft of *A History of the English-Speaking Peoples,* the main emphasis was on the national and international Press.

His range of subjects was enormous: dozens of personalities from Charlie Chaplin to Adolf Hitler, drama and books, painting, finance, history, domestic affairs, the Channel Tunnel (*plus ça change*), the House of Commons, Palestine, Ireland, Germany, Japan, Italy, America, the Spanish Civil War, Magna Carta, national sweepstakes, British Summer Time; even a collection of twelve of the world's great novels retold as short stories.[2]

And if he ranged widely in subject-matter, he was welcomed by an equally wide range of editors. Among the periodicals which published his work were: *Strand, Nash's Pall Mall, Pearsons, Saturday Review, Collier's, Cosmopolitan,* (no relation of the contemporary magazine!), *Saturday Evening Post, Atlantic, Century, Windsor;* among the newspapers: *Sunday Times, Sunday Pictorial, Sunday Dispatch, Sunday Chronicle, News of the World, Daily Mirror, Daily Telegraph, Morning Post, Daily Mail.*

And his fees were at all times equally impressive.

'His long association with *The Strand Magazine* was assumed to have begun with the publication in 1908 of a series of nine articles, *My African Journey*....He received £150 per article and £30 for the photographs which were supplied as illustrations; more than Kipling, whom *The Strand* were paying £90 for his short stories; more than W. W. Jacobs, whose rate at the time was £110 for a story.'[3]

During the First World War *The London Magazine* paid him either £3000 or £5000 (contemporary reports vary) for a series of six articles (see note 1); while after the Second World War Time-Life offered a staggering £20,000 for four short articles. ('But it's no use,' said Churchill. 'The Government would take it all. I'm not going to work when they take nineteen and six out of every pound I earn.'[4])

The syndication of articles was also impressive; indeed, it could on occasions be said to be remarkable: several articles originally published in *Nash's Pall Mall* in the late Twenties, for instance, re-appeared in the *Sunday Chronicle* during the early Thirties under different titles and prefaced by the less than accurate statement that they were 'exclusively written' for that paper. This was one result of a deliberate and surprising policy on Churchill's part, and the matter is discussed in detail in Appendix IV.

One episode vividly and amusingly illustrates the author's ever-present opportunism. In December, 1931, he was in New York and, on the evening of the 13th, set out on foot to visit a friend. Trying to cross Fifth Avenue, he was hit by a car and rushed to hospital. With astonishing *sang-froid* he quickly dictated his version of the accident and sold it to the North American Newspaper Alliance for $2500. Not only that, but he wrote the piece with an almost ghoulish relish.

'The car weighed some 2400 pounds. With my evening coat on I could not have weighed much less than 200 pounds. Taking the rate of the car at 35mph − I think a moderate estimate − I had actually to absorb in my body 6000 foot-pounds. It was the equivalent of falling 30 feet on to a pavement. The energy absorbed, though not, of course, the application of destructive force, was the equivalent of stopping ten pounds of buckshot dropped 600 feet, or two charges of buckshot at point-blank range. I do not understand why I was not broken like an egg-shell, or squashed like a gooseberry.'[5]

Not all the syndications were in the upper financial bracket, though. Kenneth Young has recorded how Churchill was 'tremendously pleased with his *Evening Standard* articles, which now syndicate to twenty-five European papers....He gets ten shillings a time from the *Malta Chronicle*.'[6]

During the Thirties particularly, Churchill's literary earnings were high by any standards, though he had yet to approach the level that they achieved after 1945. One of his secretaries of the period, Phyllis Moir, has stated that 'his books have sold amazingly well, well enough to bring him in, together with his journalistic earnings, an income of about $100,000 a year [approximately £20,000 at the time]....The advance payments made to Mr. Churchill have been among the largest in publishing history for the type of books he writes. He has always been hard up and any publisher who wanted a book from him had to be generous in the matter of advance. He does not haggle about money matters but knows exactly what he wants and generally gets it without argument.'[7]

In a parallel statement, Lord Moran recorded Churchill as saying of the Thirties, 'I was quite happy at Chartwell. I was making £20,000 every year by my books and by journalism.'[8] Given the value of money in those days, one can only take Phyllis Moir's phrase 'hard up' as relative.

Churchill published four books deriving from his early war correspondence. Five more were to come from his later journalism.

The first of these, *My African Journey*, offers an interesting example of his exploitation of a situation. When, in 1907, he decided to visit East Africa during his Under-Secretaryship of State for the Colonies, he received an offer from *The Strand* of £750 for five articles on his tour. 'I propose to accept it,' he wrote to his brother on 17 November, 'as it will definitely liquidate all possible expenses in this journey. There will be another £500 in book form.' He then handed the matter over to his then literary agent, A.P. Watt, who reported back to him on 9 January, 1908:

'I am very pleased to be able to tell you that I have succeeded in selling...the two additional pieces to which you refer on the same terms as before viz., £150 a piece....I have informed Mr Smith[9] that for the

80

£1050 which he has now agreed to pay us, you will give him 35,000 words of matter divided into eight articles....

'With regard to the book rights, Mr Smith desires me to say that he would be very glad if, in consideration of their having bought the serial rights, you would authorise us to give them the first refusal of the book rights for Messrs Hodder and Stoughton.'[10]

This agreement was concluded, with the proviso that Churchill should add an extra 10,000 words for the Hodder and Stoughton text. In the event, as I have already indicated, *The Strand* published nine articles.

The result bubbles with Churchill's irrepressible interest in everything new, whether it was the thrill of hunting rhino, the dangers of sleeping sickness, or the engagingly extempore justice of the District Officers. Characteristically, he viewed the awesome sight of the Ripon Falls not only with an aesthetic but also with a shrewdly practical eye.

'The Nile springs out of the Victorian Nyanza, a vast body of water nearly twice as wide as the Thames at Westminster Bridge, and this imposing river rushes down a stairway of rock from fifteen to twenty feet deep, in smooth, swirling slopes of green water. It would be perfectly easy to harness the whole river and let the Nile begin its beneficent journey to the sea by leaping through a turbine. It is possible that nowhere else in the world could so enormous a mass of water be held up by so little masonry.'[11]

Although twenty-two years intervened before the publication of *My Early Life*, the similarity of atmosphere is remarkable − the same sunny relaxation is present on every page, the same humour, the same considered and felicitous style. And, as in the later book, he was pleasantly willing to poke fun at himself − as when, in a moment of misguided curiosity, he prodded his walking-stick at a column of soldier ants.

'Their surprise, their confusion, their indignation were extreme. but not for an instant did they pause. In a second the scouts were running all over my boots eagerly seeking an entry, and when I looked back from this to the walking-stick I held it was already live. With a gesture so nimble that it might have been misunderstood, I cast it from me and jumped back out of the danger circle until I found refuge on a large rock at a respectful distance. The Soudanese sergeant-major of the escort, a splendid negro, drilled as smart as a Grenadier Guardsman and with a good long row of medal ribbons on his khaki tunic, so far forgot himself as to grin from ear to ear. But his gravity was fully restored when I invited him to rescue my walking-stick.'[12]

Although the main reasons for the trip were to hunt big game and to gather information at first hand, such was Churchill's personality that the semi-official visit rapidly turned into something approaching a royal progress; as the Secretary of State for the Colonies, Lord Elgin, sourly observed; 'the course is strewn with memoranda'.

Perhaps surprisingly, *My African Journey* is a far-seeing document. Lord Elgin described most of Churchill's ideas as hopelessly impracticable, but they were by no means purely visionary; his thoughts of harnessing Ripon Falls achieved reality almost sixty years later. He was also quickly aware of the potential racial problems, particularly with regard to the then emerging Asian immigrants (a problem that, decades later, became intolerable to Idi Amin), and he discussed them with a freedom and a bluntness that caused some embarrassment at the Colonial Office.

> 'In truth the problems of East Africa are the problems of the world. We see the social, racial and economic stresses which rack modern society already at work here, but in miniature; and if we choose to study the model when the whole engine is at hand, it is because on the smaller scale we see more clearly, and because in East Africa and Uganda the future is still uncompromised. The British Government has it in its hands to shape the development and destiny of these countries and their varied peoples with an authority and from an elevation far superior to that with which Cabinets can cope with their giant tangles at home. And the fact stirs the mind.'

And again, in a passage that emphasizes yet again the extreme nature of his radicalism:

> 'Indeed, it would be hard to find a country where the conditions were more favourable than in Uganda to a practical experiment in State Socialism. The land is rich; the people pacific and industrious. There are no great differences between class and class. One staple article of food meets the needs of the whole population, and produces itself almost without the aid of man. There are no European vested interests to block the way. Nowhere are the powers of the Government to regulate and direct the activities of the people more overwhelming or more

comprehensive. The superiority of knowledge in the rulers is commanding....

'It might at any rate be worth while to make such an experiment, if only as a prelude to those more general applications of the principles of Socialism which are held in some quarters to be so necessary.'

Much has happened in Uganda since 1908, but a surprising proportion of Churchill's words still hold relevance today, which is as much a criticism of successive governments as it is a compliment to the book. It has been reprinted several times in both hardback and paperback forms since its original appearance in December, 1908, when 12,500 were printed.

The Twenties were for Churchill a period of much journalistic activity, and 1932 saw the publication of *Thoughts and Adventures*, a collection of general interest features ranging from his wartime experiences in the front line to his famous pair of essays 'Hobbies' and 'Painting as a Pastime', which were later (1948) to be published in book form under the latter title. Some of them harked back to his days as First Lord of the Admiralty. Originally written in the Twenties for such magazines as *Nash's Pall Mall*, they tended to be apologias — well-argued, cogent apologias, to be sure, but noticeably defensive.

Then there were the lighter essays —'My Spy Story', for instance, a not-very-serious exercise in instant counter-espionage, and his own view of 'The Battle of Sidney Street'. Indeed, many of these articles (to use the author's own phrase) 'touch on the lighter side of grave affairs', but he went to especial pains to emphasize the seriousness of his two considerations of the future: 'Shall We All Commit Suicide?' and 'Fifty Years Hence'. 'They are offered,' he wrote, 'in deadly earnest as a warning of what may easily come to pass if Civilisation cannot take itself in hand and turn its back on those Cities of Destruction and Enslavement to which Science holds the key.'

'Shall We All Commit Suicide?' is sombrely pessimistic, and concludes with a quite breath-taking series of speculations in which Churchill foresees the development of nuclear weapons, guided missiles and militarily-deployed lasers.

'A vista opens out of electrical rays which could paralyse the engines of a motor-car, could claw down aeroplanes from the sky, and conceivably be made destructive of human life or human vision. Then there are

Explosives. Have we reached the end? Has Science turned the last pages on them? May there not be methods of using explosive energy incomparably more intense than anything heretofore discovered? Might not a bomb no bigger than an orange be found to possess a secret power to destroy a whole block of buildings – nay, to concentrate the force of a thousand tons of cordite and blast a township at a stroke? Could not explosives even of the existing type be guided automatically in flying-machines by wireless or other rays, without a human pilot, in ceaseless procession upon a hostile city, arsenal, camp or dockyard?'[13]

Let me point it up: that article was written in 1924!

'Fifty Years Hence' is scarcely less startling in its depressingly accurate vision. In it Churchill darkly foresees the advent of *in vitro* conception, genetic engineering and brainwashing techniques.

> 'It will be possible to carry out in artificial surroundings the entire cycle which now leads to the birth of a child. Interference with the mental development of such beings, expert suggestion and treatment in the earlier years, would produce beings specialised to thought or toil....A being might be produced capable of tending a machine but without other ambitions.'

To those – and there are many – who view him as a materialistic and agnostic self-seeking politician, evoking God only as a rhetorical device, Churchill's answer to the threats of an unfettered Science may come as a surprise.

> 'It is therefore above all things important that the moral philosophy and spiritual conceptions of men and nations should hold their own against these formidable evolutions. It would be much better to call a halt in material progress and discovery rather than to be mastered by our own apparatus and the forces which it directs. There are secrets too mysterious for man in his present state to know; secrets which once penetrated may be fatal to human happiness and glory....Projects undreamed of by past generations will absorb our immediate descendants; forces terrible and devastating will be in their hands; comforts, activities, amenities, pleasures will crowd upon them, but their hearts will ache, their lives will be barren, if they have not a vision above material things.'

To contemporary readers, Churchill's self-defensive insistence that these two articles be taken seriously is surely unnecessary. (Or is it?) His prophecies of our present society were astonishingly accurate, and, as with other, later, warnings, they were ignored or dismissed as mere alarmism.[14]

Or, ironically, perhaps as mere journalism.

These two essays stand out in what is otherwise an essentially lightweight book, lacking on the one hand the cohesion of *Great Contemporaries* and on the other the sheer passion of *Step by Step*. Generally amusing and often enlightening, consistently good reading, it is perhaps too arbitrary in its selection of material to pull its full weight in the Churchill canon, in spite of a sufficiency of personal revelation. Only the two articles quoted demonstrate the author's continuing use of words as weapons. Nevertheless, *Thoughts and Adventures* has contrived to remain in print fairly consistently since the original edition of 4000 copies appeared on 13 November, 1932.

One matter of minor interest is perhaps worth noting. According to Christopher Hassall in his biography of Sir Edward Marsh, the preface to this book was actually written by Marsh while Churchill was indisposed. Stylistically, it is doubtful whether anyone would ever have known: '... now confusion, uncertainty and peril, the powers of light and darkness perhaps in counterpoise, with Satan and Michael doubtfully reviewing their battalions...' One can only admire the quality of the pastiche.

However, that very quality must give rise to certain questions, and these are discussed in Appendix IV.

If the Twenties were years of intensive journalistic effort for Churchill, the Thirties saw an even more tremendous output. In 1935, apart from his other activities, he published 43 articles in British and American magazines, quite a few of them appearing on both sides of the Atlantic. In other words, there was barely a week in that year when he did not publish a full-length feature article. In 1938 the figure was 49; in 1939 the total was 35 up to the outbreak of war.

Many of the later pieces concentrated on the related problems of the growing threat of Nazism and the lack of British military preparedness, though he also kept a watchful eye on the activities of Italy, Japan and Russia. They were written in a steadily-mounting *crescendo* and *accelerando* as the decade drew towards its close, and they represent the most sustained literary campaign of his life. Indeed, he established a considerable part of his claim to the Prime Ministership through these articles; if his onslaught in the House brought him, eventually, the House's support, his Press campaign went a long way towards gaining him the people's support.

He had seen the danger of another war with Germany even before the first had entered its final phase. In articles published in both America and Britain during 1917, he insisted even then on far-reaching efforts to meet those German demands that were justifiable — demands which had led to the war that was still in progress and which, he saw, would inevitably lead to another if they were not satisfied. He also advocated a policy which foreshadowed the sentiments to be found in the 'Moral' of *The Second World War* ('In victory: magnanimity'), but which he had also broadly propounded for South Africa even before the Boer War. In the *Illustrated Sunday Herald* of 23 November, 1919, he wrote clearly and courageously to a country that had only recently been baying for the hanging of the Kaiser.

'The reconstruction of the economic life of Germany is essential to our own peace and prosperity. We do not want a land of broken, scheming, disbanded armies, putting their hands to the sword because they cannot find the spade or the hammer. The power of Britain to guide Germany into a safe channel of development and pacific recovery is considerable. We do not know how great is our power for good these days. It is a considerable opportunity in our hands. Do not let us miss it. Our safety depends on it.'

At intervals during the Twenties, Churchill had hammered away at this theme, interspersing it with warnings about growing international tensions. When Hitler came to power in 1933 Churchill immediately recognized that here was a man who would release and spearhead the frustrations of the German people. And while he produced a great deal of general writing, the majority of his journalism, indeed of his life's efforts, from then until the outbreak of war was directed towards alerting the country to a now-specific danger and towards a rapprochement with Hitler. In sharp contrast to still commonly-held beliefs, Churchill was appealing for peaceful negotiations as late as August, 1939; it could be said with some truth, indeed, that in his own way he went almost as far towards appeasement as Neville Chamberlain.

On 19 August, 1939, he published an article in *Picture Post*, the text of which appeared in both English and German. In it he wrote, showing remarkable consistency with his words of almost twenty years earlier in the *Illustrated Sunday Herald*: 'I have said repeatedly that it is a major interest of Great Britain that there should be in Europe a prosperous and happy Germany, taking an honoured and leading part in the forward guidance of the world. I look forward across the many uncertainties and dangers of these years to the day when this hope will be realised; and I am confident that that is the spirit which animates the great Parties in this island.'

And five days later − only ten days before the outbreak of war − he wrote in the unlikely pages of the *Daily Mirror*:

'But the choice is still open. There is no truth and no sense in the plea that Hitler has gone too far to stop. He could stop now. By a single impulse of will-power he could regain the solid foundations of health and sanity. He has but to send his reservists to their homes, and his example would be followed step by step in every country. He has but to restore to the Czech nation the freedom, the independence, and the frontiers he solemnly promised at Munich, to bring about an immediate revulsion of feeling in his favour throughout the world. Indeed, a new atmosphere would be created, in which every problem could be approached calmly and with a sincere desire to do the best for all.'

Nevertheless, Churchill was not interested in merely soft answers; at the same time as he explored possible pacific approaches to Hitler, he renewed his agitations for full rearmament as powerfully as he knew how; he was never willing to negotiate except from a position of strength. In particular, he attacked unsparingly the deficiencies in aircraft production.

'The bold pretence that all is well, and that everything is proceeding "according to plan", is found to lack confirmation at numberless individual points....The aircraft manufacturers complain that no broad layout of the British aircraft industry was made at the beginning of the expansion; that orders were given, and are given, piecemeal, in little packets; that they have never been able to prepare their works for mass production; that designs are repeatedly altered, to the delay of production, and that very often there is a gaping void between the execution of one contract and the assignment of another....

'It is now the thirty-third month since the Baldwin Government decided to triple the Royal Air Force. Why, then, is there not this copious flow?...

'The Government... have let the Air Ministry enjoy for nearly three years unlimited money and... a superabundant man-power. Yet at the end of the third year of expansion, already tardily begun, we are not overtaking the German monthly outputs. Indeed, if we may credit the allegations which are made more loudly every day, we are at the moment falling back not only relatively but even actually.'[15]

His weapons were used impartially. Not only did he castigate inefficiency and complacency at home but, in parallel with his endeavours to find a peaceful settlement, he entered into a final ferocious stage of his campaign against Hitler.

> 'The blow has been struck. Hitler, following exactly the doctrines of *Mein Kampf*, has broken every tie of good faith with the British and French statesmen who tried so hard to believe in him. The Munich Agreement which represented such great advantages for Germany has been brutally violated. Mr Chamberlain has been ill-used and affronted. The entire apparatus of confidence and goodwill which was being sedulously constructed in Great Britain has been shattered into innumerable fragments. It can never be mended while the present domination rules in Germany.'[16]

Three years before that, one of his *Strand* articles, 'The Truth about Hitler', had resulted in a formal protest from the German Embassy in London and in the banning in Germany of *The Strand*. 'Whether or not as a placatory gesture to the Foreign Office (rather than the Wilhelmstrasse), *The Strand* followed Churchill's article with one entitled "Hitler's Man of Strength", namely Ribbentrop. It was replete with photographs of him in various poses, including that of the devoted family man.'[17]

The lengthy series of articles running from March, 1936 to June, 1939, initially in the London *Evening Standard* and subsequently in the *Daily Telegraph*, was published as *Step by Step*, which appeared less than six weeks after the last *Telegraph* article. He was using every trick open to him to keep up the relentless pressure both at home and abroad, even until the very last moment. An edition of 7500 copies was published by Thornton Butterworth on 27 June, 1939, but by the time the first reprint was ordered (another 1500 copies) the country was already at war.

Step by Step is, like *Arms and the Covenant*, essentially of its day; but it still holds tremendous power. Churchill was always outstanding at arguing a case concisely, and here he employed every weapon he had learned to use during just over forty years of journalism and almost as many of politics.

It is no coincidence that two of Churchill's most powerfully-expressed books should derive from the same three-year period and be devoted to the same subject. His opposition to Nazism was virtually his entire political *raison d'être* during the Thirties, and (at least partly) because of this tenacity he was politically ostracised during those years. Yet through this same tenacity (bloody-mindedness, even) he rose to the greatest period of his life and to his lasting eminence in world history.

If, during the Twenties and Thirties, Churchill's primary journalistic efforts were devoted to warning the country of future perils, he nevertheless found time for exploring other, less demanding fields. It seems to have mattered little whether he wrote an article on the newly launched *Queen Mary* or on the Coronation of King George VI; a series of articles on 'The Great Reigns' or one on 'Great Events of our Time'; many subjects were grist to his tireless mill. Apart from anything else, he had no Cabinet salary after 1929 and it was largely his journalism that enabled him to maintain his comfortable standard of living. He therefore accepted virtually every opportunity for publication with alacrity and professionalism. Articles might have been delivered by taxi at the last possible moment, but he never missed a copy-date, even at the height of his political worries.

It is scarcely surprising, therefore, that some of his output is not of the highest quality. Features such as 'Are There Men in the Moon?' and 'Life under the Microscope' bear the unmistakable mark of the bottom drawer,[18] and others were just as clearly thrown together for the sake of the job. That on William Willett, the originator of British Summer Time, for instance, is one such; a superficial trio of articles entitled 'Parliament from the Inside' is another.

Nevertheless, it should not be thought that the majority of Churchill's journalism not reprinted during his lifetime is worthless; far from it. A surprising amount retains its interest and relevance today. Indeed, in the late 1950s, Churchill had intended to agree to the publication of a collection of such articles under the title of *The Truth about Myself and Other Essays*; only illness and age reversed his original intention.[19] It was, therefore, by no means that he himself thought that he had reprinted all that was worthy of book form. There are, indeed, some treasures.

His studies of America, for instance − as in 'Land of Corn and Lobsters' − are witty and penetrating, and even if they sometimes talk of such un-American activities as prohibition they still carry many telling and felicitous phrases, and present a lively picture of American society between the wars.

A possibly unexpected portrayal of another side of American life came earlier when he wrote an extended review of Upton Sinclair's novel about the Chicago meat industry, *The Jungle* (1906). His reception of this strongly left-wing novel of protest is one more sharp reminder of the passionate nature of his radical phase.

'It pierces the thickest skull and the most leathery heart. It forces people who never think about the foundation of society to pause and wonder. It enables those who sometimes think to understand. The justification of that vast and intricate fabric of Factory Law, of Health Acts, of Workmen's Compensation, upon which Parliament is swiftly and laboriously building year by year and month by month, is made plain, so that a child may see it, so that a fool may see it, so that a knave may see it.'[20]

His response to the request to write 'fictional history' for *Scribner's Magazine* was the virtuoso double-take of 'If Lee had not won the Battle of Gettysburg,' in which he brilliantly projected an 'alternative' course of modern American history. Some of his personality pieces such as those on Chaplin and Rockefeller, though naturally incomplete (they were written in 1935 and 1936 respectively), are full of insight and understanding. His characteristically forceful historical articles often appear now to be miniature aperitifs for his *History of the English-Speaking Peoples*: decorated with dazzling phrases, shot through with epigram, studded with encapsulated judgments that at once amuse and instruct (though there is never any guarantee of absolute objectivity!) Here, for instance, he dismisses the Stuarts in a few savage sentences:

'They never seemed to fit the English requirements. We review them all. James I, odious but crafty; Charles I, eyeing his judges with unaffected scorn; Charles II, restored his dynasty, given a second chance up-borne by the love of his people, spending it all with ladies and lap-dogs; James II, ready to run all risks, make all sacrifices, inflict all punishments to compel Protestant England to cleave again to Rome; they none of them suited England.'[21]

Hardly academic history perhaps, but splendidly entertaining in its controlled employment of intentionally unfair abuse.

But what gladiator ever fought by the Queensberry rules?

Churchill's first piece of professional journalism appeared in 1895, the year in which his father died. His last publication, entitled 'The Dream',[22] though written in 1946 or 1947, appeared posthumously in 1966, a span of over seventy years.

The first was written under the shadow of his father's vitriolic attacks ('you will degenerate into a shabby unhappy & futile existence'); in the last he turned to dispute on equal terms with his father's shade — an ironically fitting end to such a lengthy, varied and successful journalistic career.

VII

THE BIOGRAPHIES

So far we have examined Churchill as a gladiator very much out in the open, his weapons displayed and his intentions in no doubt. Whether he was fighting for personal advancement (as in the war despatches) or to consolidate a political strongpoint, the belligerence was overt. With his biographies, however, we meet him perhaps more as a member of an underground force, seeking to achieve his ends by more subtle and less direct tactics.

Here he was faced not with writing of events at first-hand, but with lengthy and demanding research; with formulating historical judgments; with achieving an air of at least apparent objectivity.

So, whereas in the field he had expressed his opinions directly and forcibly, now he adopted the air of an academic and sought to take his place at the High Table.

In doing so, he attracted public eulogy and the rancour of some professional historians who not only cited his amateur status, but also his inexperience in research and consequent lack of judgment.

These reactions, though, were still in the future. Faced with the new problem of original research, Churchill rose to the task with relish. If the approach had to be different, clearly he was confident he could make it his own. And there were still the magnificent set-pieces he loved so much; still there were courage, high endeavour, dedication, magnitude; still there were to be found in the subjects he chose justifications for that near-mythic view of English history.

Churchill wrote only two full biographies. At one time he contemplated a life of Napoleon which must be, as Maurice Ashley remarked, 'one of the great unwritten books of our time'. The other books in this genre were *My Early Life,* a racy, humorous, self-deprecating classic of autobiography which, alas, only takes the reader as far as 1900, and his collection of journalistic profiles entitled *Great Contemporaries.*

It is significant that both the biographies were of his ancestors. In each case he was spurred to the task by the belief that it was necessary to defend the subject and to correct public impressions based on misunderstanding or even deliberate malice.

Lord Randolph had departed from politics under a cloud. Always volatile, and probably already suffering from the initial stages of his tertiary syphilis, he made a fatal tactical resignation in 1886 and never held office again, dying nine years later a stricken and broken man. Misconceptions of his life and work remained; memories of earlier controversies coloured Churchill's own first steps in Parliament, to the extent that he deliberately made an early speech on the very topic that had caused his father's downfall. Clearly there was much to be done there in the way of filial piety.

In the case of Marlborough, he believed that there were deep-seated calumnies, many stemming from Macaulay's vitriolic criticisms in his *History of England* (1849-61). Having accepted these for so long, Churchill, when finally persuaded of their lack of substance, sprang to the task of rehabilitation with enthusiasm.

Lord Randolph Churchill was the first and last major work that Churchill tackled as an individual.[1] True, he relied to a considerable extent on memoranda and reminiscences from his father's friends and colleagues, but the book was very much a solo effort.

Although *Lord Randolph Churchill* did not appear until 1906, Churchill had made the project his own − mentally, at least − as early as 1899, when he wrote to his mother:

'I was interested in the cutting about Papa's biography. You must use all your influence to get the papers for me. [George] Curzon could not well refuse. The time has not yet come − but in six or seven years it will have arrived − and I shall insist on undertaking the work. G.C. may edit if he likes. I have every right and can do it much better than anyone else likely to get hold of the papers. Don't let them publish any rubbish now. I shall think you unwise if you allow it when in any way you can deter them. From a financial point of view alone − the biography would be worth £2000.'[2]

In fact Churchill had actually been approached by a publisher, Nisbet and Co, during April, 1898, when he was still stationed in India and only a few weeks after the publication of *The Malakand Field Force.* The approach was cautious in the extreme: 'How far such matters are ripe for such an undertaking, or how far it may have been arranged already, I do not of course know; & it may be that the question is one which you may not desire to open'. He did not take up this offer, but the seed was sown and he responded to the subsequent stimulus eagerly. Nevertheless, he bided his time until December, 1901, when he discussed the matter with Curzon (by then the 4th Earl Howe.) Having broached the subject, he was content to let it lie dormant again until the middle of the following year, when he wrote to Lord Rosebery.

> 'I had some talk at Christmas with George Howe about my father's papers & that I should write his life. He was quite sympathetic and has promised to consult again with you and Hicks Beach. I hope in such an event that you will feel able to encourage the idea; for I should very much like to undertake the work and would approach it with reverence and industry.....[3]

Lord Rosebery did not fail him. At the beginning of August Lord Randolph's Trustees informed him that the papers — eighteen boxes of them — were at his disposal. As his bachelor flat in London was too small, the Duke of Marlborough offered him a suite at Blenheim where he could spread himself and the thousands of documents. His brother Jack was conscripted to assist in the immense task of sorting. The papers were divided into piles, each with a note indicating the period covered. Personal papers were returned to the boxes, while the important political papers were subsequently bound by the Duke in thirty-two blue morocco volumes, stamped with the family arms in gold leaf on front and back.

Churchill faced this new problem of handling raw material with characteristic assurance.

> 'There emerges from these dusty records a great and vivid drama, and I feel at each step growing confidence that I shall be able to write what many will care to read. But I do not mean to put pen to paper until the whole of the evidence is before me, and as there are six times as many papers as those I have looked through you will understand that my days are very fully occupied....Will you send me any scrap-book you have of my Father's newspaper-cuttings, and please keep turning over in your mind any way you can help me in collecting material; all is grist that comes to my mill and the more saturated I am with the subject before I begin to write the better the work will be.'[4]

At the same time he wrote to his father's contemporaries: to

Balfour, Chamberlain, St John Brodrick and, above all, Rosebery. Most replied fully, though Rosebery vacillated oddly, first promising a memoir, then saying it had been burned, and then finally publishing it as a separate — and delightful — monograph himself.

Meanwhile the Trustees were already endeavouring to exercise more control than Churchill wished. After consulting a barrister, they wrote to him with various limiting proposals. Confronted for the first time with one of biographers' frequent hazards, Churchill fended it off with an admirable integrity and logic.

'I incline strongly to the belief that the duty of the literary executors is discharged "when to the best of their judgment they have selected a suitable biographer". Questions of style, or literary taste, of the scope of the work, of the proportion of various incidents in the work, are all matters of opinion, and matters upon which opinion will very often be divided. A syndicate may compile an encyclopedia, only a man can write a book. Once the human element in a book is destroyed by unsympathetic or foreign alterations it cannot be of any real literary excellence and its only value is to be found in the facts it records. Therefore I am of the opinion... that the fullest discretion and liberty in the treatment of the subject must be accorded to the biographer; and I am quite certain that, whatever arrangement my strong personal feeling both of desire to write this work and of friendship to you might lead me to acquiesce in, no strange writer of any literary or financial independence would undertake the task if he were "liable to have the entire work or even a whole chapter objected to".'[5]

That said, Churchill diplomatically accepted various minor conditions and work proceeded steadily over the next three years. Not all his inquiries bore fruit, however. 'I need not tell you,' wrote A. J. Balfour, 'that any letters I have from your father are entirely at your disposal. But alas I am a most disorderly person, and though I feel pretty confident that I have destroyed none, I may have some difficulty in laying my hands on them.' Lord Goschen replied with stunning honesty: 'I do not, I think, have an inaccurate memory of events: I simply forget.'[6] Almost two years later Balfour was still having difficulty in finding any letters ('This is curious...') but by the end of 1904 Churchill was writing. For the first time he employed a shorthand typist, having each chapter set up in type at his own expense and proofed as it was completed — a practice that he followed thereafter for the rest of his life. By February, 1905, he was into the second chapter and appealing to his mother for 'three or four sheets of recollections about your life in London and in Ireland with my father from 1874 to 1880.' Throughout the spring and summer, letters flowed to and fro from Churchill, questioning, arguing, discussing, probing. Galley proofs (prepared by his first publisher Longman) went to his various informants for checking, lacunae were filled, revisions made.

And on 2 October, 1905, Churchill appointed his agent − in retrospect the startlingly unlikely figure of Frank Harris,[7] afterwards to become notorious but then an established and respected London literary leader.

Churchill wrote:

> 'I authorise you as my friend to talk in confidence & privacy to publishers about my book. I reserve to myself the right to decide freely on every offer − whether as regards whole world rights, or English, foreign or Colonial rights − even to the extent of taking a lower one, if I choose. But if, as the result of your negotiations, I make a bargain then I shall pay you 10% on the excess net profit accruing to me from that bargain above £4000, as such profits may be realised.'

He also sent proofs of the book to Harris with the request: 'Please pencil whatever comments occur to you.' Harris took the request seriously but apparently found little to criticize. 'I must assure you,' he wrote on 7 October, 'that you have done a very fine & noble piece of work − out of sight better than Rosebery's *Pitt* or Morley's *Gladstone,* a book which will be as Thucydides said of his own history... "A possession for ever," something that even this English public will not willingly forget.'

Harris went about the task with his customary bustling energy. To Heinemann and Methuen he wrote: 'It is as interesting as a great novel, partly because of the extraordinary vicissitudes and tragic end of Lord Randolph Churchill's life and partly because of the masterly treatment; it is of widest appeal more especially by reason of the number of letters it contains from the Queen, from Lord Salisbury, while Prime Minister, from Mr Gladstone, from Lord Hartington, Mr Balfour, Mr Chamberlain and other eminent persons, and the light which these letters throw on the secret workings of Cabinets and Governments in this country.'[8]

There is distinct relish in Harris's letters to the publishers, and clearly he enjoyed the haggling as much as the appointment itself. Juggling simultaneously with Cassell, Heinemann, Methuen, Arnold, Macmillan, Murray and Hutchinson, he assessed and calculated, ruthlessly eliminating the weak ('From what I saw of him he is not rich enough to risk a sum like eight or ten thousand.') and gradually settling upon the offer from Macmillan. In fact the word 'gradually' is somewhat misleading, for it was only a fortnight later that Harris received the following letter from George Macmillan.

'We have read with very great interest the sheets of Mr Winston Churchill's Life of his father and understanding that he wishes to sell the book outright we are prepared to pay the sum of £7000 for the entire copyright in this country and the United States. We shall be glad to hear as soon as possible whether this offer meets Mr Churchill's views.'

Harris pushed a little harder, and five days later Frederick Macmillan, the Chairman, wrote directly to Churchill to confirm the final terms. These were remarkable by any standards. The publisher agreed to pay £8000 for English language rights and, further, 'after Macmillans have earned £4000 profits for themselves, we are to divide all further profits which may be realised during the period of legal copyright.'

Acclaim, both public and private, greeted the publication of the two volumes on 2 January, 1906. Of the 8000 copies printed, over 2300 were sold in the first week, and three-quarters of the edition by the end of April. The reviews − with one or two notable exceptions − were lengthy and appreciative. 'It is a pleasure to be able to say,' wrote the anonymous critic of *The Times Literary Supplement*, 'that a life so well worth writing has been so admirably written....No one who cares for politics will willingly put it down when it is once in his hands.' *The Sunday Times* praised its 'maturity of judgment, levelheadedness and discretion'; while *The Spectator* observed: 'He has chosen the grand manner...but the general effect is of dignity and ease.'

Letters flowed in from old friends: from Rosebery, Chamberlain, J.A. Spender, the Duke of Marlborough, Wilfred Scawen Blunt, and from the King. Of the many compliments, it is Lord Rosebery's which is the most widely quoted, doubtless because of its high terms: one of the first dozen, he said, perhaps the first half-dozen, biographies in our language. Even if this was not an overstatement in 1906 (which it might well not have been), it is certainly one now, given the sharply differing biographical and historical disciplines of more recent years. Nevertheless, *Lord Randolph Churchill* is still a prime source work and a magnificently written book. As Robert

Rhodes James acknowledged in his 1959 biography, 'It is a formidable undertaking to follow'.

On the surface it is probably the most objective of Churchill's books; it *reads* like a straightforward, balanced appraisal, and would certainly have seemed such to most of its contemporary audience. In the Preface he wrote: 'I have thought it my duty, so far as possible, to assemble once and for all the whole body of historical evidence required for the understanding of Lord Randolph Churchill's career. Scarcely anything of material consequence has been omitted, and such omissions as have been necessary are made for others' sakes and not his own. Scarcely any statement of importance lacks documentary proof. There is nothing more to tell. Wherever practicable I have endeavoured to use his own words in the narration; and the public is now in a position to pronounce a complete, if not a final, judgment.'

Here already, before the telling has even begun, there are clear warning signs: 'so far as possible', 'scarcely anything', 'scarcely any statement' – these qualifications should immediately alert the reader to the probability of evasions to follow. And there was certainly 'more to tell'. Churchill was never an objective writer by intention, but now the distortions are more subtle than before, the result of a newly-acquired skill in the discreet massaging of unwelcome facts.

It is not my basic purpose here to assess the overall historical and biographical aspects of the works under discussion; it is rather to consider how Churchill used his writings to achieve specific predetermined aims. Here his overt aim was to write a definitive life of his father; his covert aim was to rehabilitate him. The two are not necessarily inclusive.

Clearly, the fact that he was Lord Randolph's son immediately – and particularly in the context of the period – imposed restraints, to go against which would have been considered a major social solecism. Further, and equally (if not more) importantly, the fledgling politician had to work with many of those who had been his father's colleagues and opponents, and who were now capable of exercising a crucial influence for good or ill on his parliamentary career; this too imposed significant restraints of which he was only too aware, as he had already demonstrated by his self-imposed censorship of his attacks on Kitchener in *The River War*.

These were both powerful imperatives, but I do not believe that they were the main forces in his presentation. In spite of his father's coldness towards him, Churchill believed passionately in him and in what he had achieved during his short life. Lord Randolph had fallen disastrously, and his son felt driven to restore the earlier lustre.

So, flying in the face of his prefatory statement of integrity, he set about the deliberate process of reconstruction. 'It was,' as Plumb wrote, 'a justification of a life, an act of piety, not an historical assessment.' And yet, for Churchill, it was what he desired as an historical assessment. Perhaps he even believed it truly was.

Lord Randolph's letters were often ungrammatical, laced with contractions and abbreviations; the product of a mind in top gear. From about 1892, as his syphilis began to tighten its fatal hold, they became even more eccentric than they habitually were, and this was one reason why Churchill tidied up the documents he published, an action acknowledged only in the phrase '*Wherever practicable* [my italics] I have endeavoured to use his own words'. This, if it were merely for the sake of clarity and smooth reading, would be defensible, though modern disciplines would demand otherwise; but Churchill also took the opportunity silently to omit whole passages. These omissions, he said in the Preface, were 'made for others' sakes'.

But in his most elegant memoir Lord Rosebery suggested another possible motive: 'If there be a flaw, if there be a want unsatisfied, it is perhaps that we are not treated to more of Randolph's crisp, pointed, and delightful letters. The reason is, no doubt that they were too crisp, pointed, and delightful for present publication.'[9]

At the risk of labouring an already obvious point, Rosebery's language (itself crisp, pointed and delightful) is clearly euphemistic as well as gently tongue-in-cheek. What he is actually saying, of course, is that a lot of Lord Randolph's letters were downright libellous in their uncensored form. Churchill's statement that the omissions were made 'for others' sakes' supports that interpretation of Rosebery's delicate jibe.

Even if one grants that the omissions were made at least partly for the reason given by Churchill, it is nevertheless undeniable that such omissions also had the effect of masking the often cruelly abrasive aspect of Lord Randolph's character, a side that Churchill himself knew only too well. The edited texts are altogether too bland and represent a distortion that must have been accepted by Churchill, if not positively sought, for who better than the author could recognize the difference between the original and revised texts?

Perhaps one can go even further and ask whether his primary motive was, as expressed, 'for others' sakes,' or to present his father in a better light. The dark side of Lord Randolph's personality was widely known both inside and outside Parliament. Queen Victoria described him in her journal as 'so mad and odd'; Lord Ripon called him 'an unprincipled mountebank'. Lord Salisbury's view was that 'the Mahdi[10] pretends to be half-mad and is very sane in reality; Lord Randolph occupies exactly the converse position.' Even the gentle Rosebery felt compelled to record the hostility with which Lord Randolph was regarded in his lifetime. 'To many excellent persons, both Tory and Liberal, Randolph was little less than an incarnation of evil, a reckless and insolent iconoclast; a conspirator against the fathers of his own political creed, while outraging and insulting the venerable chiefs of the other. He was, in their judgment, unscrupulous, violent, unprincipled; an intriguing schemer, a ruthless plotter; one who, to serve the personal ambition which was his sole motive, would stick at nothing.'[11]

Views such as those were more or less privately expressed at the time, but on the publication of the biography the *Daily Telegraph* reviewer was just as outspoken, so much so that the incensed Duke of Marlborough forced a retraction.

'Fortunately, Lord Randolph Churchill has been allowed to tell his own story in these 1000 pages. The record of his career, stripped of the glosses, suggestions, and inferences with which Mr Churchill naturally seeks to clothe it, is plain enough for the public to understand....

'His character, his temperament, and a certain intellectual obliquity of vision prevented him from making permanent and beneficial use of powers which were unquestionably very remarkable. Only those who knew him personally could describe the curious fascination which he exercised over those brought into contact with him, and they could not explain it. His treatment of his friends was often atrocious, sometimes not even honourable; he was very careless of the truth, and he did things for which other men would almost have been ostracised.'[12]

There was, therefore, ample reason for Churchill to believe that his father's image needed a great deal of refurbishing. Lord Randolph may have excited universal pity in the manner of his 'dying by inches in public', but that had done little, if anything, to eradicate the widespread antagonism that he had created during his career. If Churchill was to rehabilitate his father for future generations, he had to counter the many prevailing memories of spitefulness, acerbity, derision, sarcasm, high-handedness, duplicity and, to one person at least, downright treachery.

By toning down his father's letters and other documents, Churchill went some way towards meeting this problem. Is it possible, then, to regard such an apparently innocent editorial decision as ingenuously as Churchill (perhaps disingenuously) offers it? Young though he still was, he was neither a political virgin nor a literary tyro.

If some doubt has been thrown on the apparent objectivity of *Lord Randolph Churchill*, more must surely accrue even from a neutral consideration of other aspects of the book, especially those relating to the Fourth Party, his extraordinary betrayal of Louis Jennings in 1890, his behaviour with regard to Home Rule, and his speech on that subject in February, 1893.

The Fourth Party consisted of precisely four people: Lord Randolph, A.J. Balfour, Harold Gorst and Sir Henry Drummond Wolff.[13] It was, in fact, no more than an iconoclastic splinter-group dedicated to nagging its own party leaders and motivated largely by Lord Randolph's own driving ambitions. Churchill made much of its independence and its positive contribution to both debates and policy; yet Rosebery, who had known Lord Randolph since their childhood days at Eton, gave a colder and more rational appraisal, a view all the more salutory for being included in his friendly, even loving, memoir.

> 'It was indeed originally an escapade, carried out with high spirits and with the tongue often in the cheek. As it prospered, it became formidable and therefore serious; yet it embodied nothing but a negative. Its aim was to oppose, hinder, thwart, and wreck the work of the Government in every possible way.'[14]

The Fourth Party, in effect, consisted of four rebellious young politicians who hoped to make their reputations: Lord Randolph through his own efforts, the others through association with him. At no time was it other than self-seeking; its contribution to government was non-existent, except in the personal sense that Lord Randolph achieved brief Cabinet rank and Balfour, in the longer term, a more permanent eminence (though an equally dubious reputation).

If Churchill sought to make more of the Fourth Party than is justified, he sought to make little of the extraordinary episode in 1890 which led to the permanent break between Lord Randolph and his long-standing friend and colleague Louis Jennings, over the debate on the Resolution regarding the findings of the Special

Commission on the Parnell affair. The convolutions of his behaviour are so strange that, as with his earlier resignation, one can only ascribe them to the working of his disease.

Having himself suggested that Jennings should table an amendment emphasizing the total acquittal of Parnell, and actually written it himself, he then, two days later, told Jennings, 'It is a mistake; can't be defended'. Jennings was both amazed and disheartened by this *volte-face* but nonetheless determined to proceed.

Immediately before the debate Curzon informed Jennings that Lord Randolph intended not to support the amendment in the House, and added, 'Randolph will not take any part in the debate unless you are attacked.'

In spite of this undertaking, Lord Randolph surreptitiously arranged with the Speaker to be called, even after one amendment had been voted on. Preceding Jennings, he delivered a speech that at times bordered on the hysterical ('the bloody, rotten, ghastly foetus, Piggott, Piggott, Piggott'[15]), culminating in the thinly-veiled and paranoic suggestion that the Government might use a Piggott-figure against him or anyone else who dared to oppose it. Disgusted both by the intervention and its contents, made against all Lord Randolph's undertakings to the contrary, Jennings refused to put his amendment forward. Lord Randolph's protestations of surprised innocence ring hollowly and shabbily even in his son's account.

Immediately afterwards, Jennings wrote a memorandum regarding the episode which was eventually published as an appendix to the biography. While its inclusion might be taken as an indication of Churchill's scrupulous fairness, he endeavoured to nullify its effect by printing a contrary statement that he had requested especially from Lord Justice Fitzgibbon, who had been involved in discussions prior to the debate. Its value, however, must surely be diminished by its having been written nearly fifteen years after the event, whereas Jennings' account was contemporaneous.

A small point — perhaps, some might say, even a quibble — but there is no doubt that Churchill was contriving as best he could to throw doubt upon the facts. This is going beyond honesty, towards the grey areas of disinformation.

Lord Randolph's position over Home Rule was one of total opposition, yet in practice some of his actions and attitudes were, to say the least, ambivalent. In spite of his beliefs he negotiated a secret arrangement with Parnell, trading off a relatively minor concession (the dropping of the Coercion Bill, which stood little chance of getting through Parliament anyway) in return for the Irish vote at the next election, and then denying the existence of any agreement; the best one can say is that his denial was not made in the House. And while maintaining friendly contact with Parnell through Captain O'Shea, he was at the same time receiving reports seeking proof of Parnell's direct involvement with Phoenix Park.

He was also capable of saying (in November, 1885) 'those foul Ulster Tories have always ruined our party. I am afraid it is too late to remedy the evil'; yet within four months he deliberately whipped up those same Ulster Tories with a speech that Churchill astonishingly claims was made 'without using language of bigotry or intolerance'. The following is the peroration of the address, made in Belfast on 22 February, 1886:

> '...if it should turn out that the Parliament of the United Kingdom was so recreant from all its high duties, and that the British nation was so apostate to traditions of honour and courage, as to hand over the Loyalists of Ireland to the domination of an Assembly in Dublin which must be to them a foreign and an alien assembly, if it should be within the design of Providence to place upon you and your fellow-Loyalists so heavy a trial, then, gentlemen, I do not hesitate to tell you most truly that in that dark hour there will not be wanting to you those of position and influence in England who would be willing to cast in their lot with you and who, whatever the result, will share your fortunes and your fate. There will not be wanting those who at the exact moment, when the time is fully come — if that time should come — will address you in words which are perhaps best expressed by one of our greatest English poets:-
>
> > 'The combat deepens; on, ye brave,
> > Who rush to glory or the grave.
> > Wave, Ulster — all thy banners wave
> > And charge with all thy chivalry.'[16]

Not bigotry? Not intolerance? Perhaps it depends on how you define the words; but there can be little doubt that the speech was blatantly inflammatory, a considered incitement to violence. Yet Churchill passes over it blandly, only pausing to note the fact that Lord Salisbury wrote encouragingly to Lord Randolph on the following day: 'I thought it singularly skilful...I am sure the effect of the speech will be very great in Ulster.'

Lord Randolph, however, was clearly aware of the enormity of what he had said and done. In his reply to Salisbury on 24 February he said, 'If I am put upon my trial for high treason, I shall certainly rely on yr evidence that at any rate up to the 22nd of this month my action was constitutional.'

In spite of the vast quantity of documents and letters published in Churchill's book, this one does not appear. Filial piety or blatant *suppressio veri*?

Very shortly after that speech, in a letter to a Liberal-Unionist MP, Lord Randolph went even further and, interestingly, Churchill unconsciously gives the lie to his earlier disclaimer.

> '...*he repeated his menace in an even clearer form:* [my italics] "If political parties and political leaders...should be so utterly lost to every feeling and dictate of honour and courage as to hand over coldly, and for the sake of purchasing a short and illusory Parliamentary tranquillity, the lives and liberties of the Loyalists of Ireland to their hereditary and most bitter foes, make no doubt on this point − Ulster will not be a consenting party; Ulster at the proper moment will resort to the supreme arbitrament of force; Ulster will fight, Ulster will be right." '

'The supreme arbitrament of force': the call to violence is unmistakable, yet Churchill passes over it with a positively Nelsonian eye as being, apparently, unworthy of discussion or even comment.

One further matter deserves attention, and that is Churchill's treatment of his father's speech on the Home Rule Bill in 1893. This was the speech that publicly marked the end of his parliamentary life and which devastated the House by its horror. Churchill wrote:

> 'It seemed incredible that this bald and bearded man with shaking hands and a white face drawn with pain and deeply marked with the lines of care and illness, and with a voice whose tremulous tones already betrayed the fatal difficulty of articulation, could be that same brilliant audacious leader who in the flush of exultant youth had marched irresistibly to power through the stormy days of 1886.
>
> 'Yet the quality of his speech showed no signs of intellectual failing. Avoiding the network of details in which so many speakers had stumbled, he presented a broad intelligible picture. Lucid and original expression, close and careful reasoning, wealth of knowledge, quaint Randolphian witticisms − all were there. Although much of the charm and force of his manner was gone, his statement was considered by

good and impartial judges to have been, with the exception of Mr Chamberlain's, the best speech delivered on the Bill.'[17]

Rosebery disagreed sadly but profoundly, and he, unlike Churchill, had been present at that harrowing debate. Against Churchill's second-hand reconstruction, Rosebery's first-hand and extremely moving memory bears the stamp of truth. Having quoted Churchill's words (as above), he went on:

> 'Each must speak for himself. It may have been so, but I am sure the audience did not realise the fact. To them and to the orator it was one long pain − pain of watching and listening, pain of thick and almost unintelligible delivery, pain of memory and contrast, pain for the visible imminence of death. What the speech may have been none who heard it know; for it was a waking nightmare.'

And he continued inexorably:

> 'He went on making speeches; addressing audiences in the country with restless courage; and returned to London declaring that he had never held such meetings. This was the hallucination of disease. Great audiences came indeed to hear him once more, but they could no longer catch his half-articulated words, and soon went away in sorrow and astonishment. But this, happily, he did not realise.'[18]

Rosebery's final words are surely the epitome of sympathy and understanding.

Which report does one accept? That written from hearsay and familial partisanship thirteen years after the event, or that deriving from a loving, grieving and personal observation? And what were Churchill's thoughts, one wonders, when Rosebery's version came out so hard on the heels of his own?

One day in 1892 Lord Randolph had a rare talk with his young son, in the course of which he said, 'My every action is misjudged and every word distorted....So make some allowances.'[19] Clearly Churchill took the plea to heart, deaf to its overtones of paranoia.

For one significant piece of factual massaging we can surely forgive him: his avoidance of the fact of his father's syphilis. Even in this present generation, let alone the Victorian and Edwardian eras, one would have to have little regard (perhaps even much hate) for either family or self to broadcast such a fact to the world at large.

Nevertheless, his explanation must strike the modern reader as bordering on the naive.

> 'The great strain to which he had subjected himself during the struggle with Mr Gladstone, the vexations and disappointments of later years and finally the severe physical exertion and exposure of South Africa had produced in a neurotic temperament and delicate constitution a very rare and ghastly disease.'

With hindsight, it is a little difficult to understand how Churchill got away with this extraordinary statement: strain, vexation and exertion cannot result in a *disease*. But get away with it he did, to the extent that Robert Rhodes James repeated the final phrase in his 1959 biography without even putting it in quotation marks, while the official biography (1966) merely refers to 'a severe mental disease'.

But if that suppression is understandable, it must be recognized that it inevitably led to inadequacies of interpretation, since only in the light of the early symptoms of tertiary syphilis do some of Lord Randolph's actions make sense, in particular, that catastrophically ill-judged resignation of 1886.

As we have seen, Churchill was personally in a difficult situation if he did not wish to antagonize his parliamentary superiors. His final summing-up, therefore, was a minor masterpiece of insinuation. There were too many vested interests still in politics, too many yes-men, too many self-deluding hypocrites ready to sacrifice anything to the dictates of the Party or their own advancement. Yet there were also untainted men; let Lord Randolph therefore be judged by them; not merely judged but (implicitly, for the first time) 'justly' judged.

> 'There is an England which stretches far beyond the well-drilled masses who are assembled by party machinery to salute with appropriate acclamation the utterances of their recognised fuglemen; an England of wise men who gaze without self-deception at the failings and follies of both political parties; of brave and earnest men who find in neither faction fair scope for the effort that is in them; of "poor men" who increasingly doubt the sincerity of party philanthropy. It was to that England that Lord Randolph Churchill appealed; it was that England he so nearly won; it is by that England he will be justly judged.'[20]

Apart from the specific distortions of intent, it must also be said that the biography is flawed in another way too: the complex personality of Lord Randolph is nowhere to be seen. Nowhere is any light thrown on his 'curious fascination', his undoubted charisma. As Frank Harris observed, '...of the man himself, his powers, his failings and quiddities, hardly a self-revealing word'.

The reason is, I think, clear enough: Churchill simply did not know his father as a person. Nevertheless, the lack is crucial, even though it is counterbalanced by Lord Rosebery's monograph, also published in 1906. But Churchill was never one to spin psychological webs, or pry too deeply into cupboards. 'He is content to survey the upper portions of the iceberg which is human personality, and to leave the four-fifths under the water largely unexplored....It may be doubted whether Sir Winston would even now feel constrained, or even see any necessity, to fill in the large blank spaces in his portraiture.'[21] Not for him the portrayal warts and all, the analytical picking-over of superficies. He held even then to the grand gesture, the brilliant panoramic canvas, the imagination-catching legend. He could never summon up the necessary detachment to become a truly great historian. Involvement was one of his great strengths but it led him, here as elsewhere, into an unevenness of vision.

Successful biographies of fathers by sons are rare enough; given the specifics of this one it is remarkable that Churchill was as successful as he was. In spite of its self-inflicted wounds and other flaws, the book still has great value. It will remain a source of biographers and political historians, and it will also remain, from the literary point of view, an outstanding piece of writing.

Churchill was now an experienced politician. He had learned that the truth is malleable, and this book is the first literary evidence of that lesson. In a personal sense, it served two purposes: it helped to lay a ghost, and it opened up a new dimension for his literary career.

Whereas Churchill's public stance regarding *Lord Randolph Churchill* was one of apparent impartiality, it was breathtakingly different when he came to *Marlborough*; indeed, it is a vivid example of the theory that it is the converts who believe most passionately.

When Charles Mallet of Nisbet and Co. had written to Churchill in April, 1898, he had proposed not just a memoir of Lord Randolph but also − and primarily − one of Marlborough.

'This firm is beginning to publish a series of volumes of historical biography, volumes of some 100,000 words, intended to deal fully, & in a method both scholarly and picturesque, with certain great historical figures, whose lives have not been adequately treated yet. A suggestion has been made to include in such a series a life of the great Duke of Marlborough which would not compete with Coxe's or Lord Wolseley's but which would yet cover the subject effectively & well. I do not know whether your inclinations have ever led you to contemplate work of this kind, or whether you would care to consider the possibility of undertaking such a task.'

With no signs of his later antagonism towards the Duke, Churchill considered this with rather more immediacy than the other proposition, and on 16 May wrote to his mother:

'It is necessary to find out
(1) Whether the publishers are a good firm.
(2) Their terms.
(3) Whether Sunny [the then Duke of Marlborough] objects.
(4) Whether it would be correct literary etiquette for one to publish a work while Ld Wolseley's books on the same subject are still under construction.
(5) You might even find out what he would think of the matter − if you see him. Though as he would not be C in C when I publish − it could make no difference. He has never done anything for me. Still I don't want to poach.'

And at the end of a very long letter to his mother only six days later he wrote (with rather less consideration for Wolseley):

'The "Marlborough" idea gains strength every day in my mind. I think I could produce a wonderful book. Wolseley's is deadly.'

Nisbet tried again in 1899 but Churchill took the matter no further until 1928 when, in a cautious letter to his wife, he wrote:

'A.P. Watt, my first literary agent, came yesterday with a proposal for a Life of the Duke of Marlborough, for which £8000 was guaranteed on account of royalties in England and America. He indicated that a better offer would probably be forthcoming. This would be a long job but it certainly lies in the future, and no doubt better terms could be obtained.'[22]

They certainly could. Churchill, acting as his own agent, negotiated a far better contract with Harrap, by which he received £10,000 for the British Empire book rights alone, plus a $5,000 advance from Scribner for the American rights. He also sold the first serial rights to *The Sunday Times* which subsequently (1938) awarded the work its Gold Medal.

Having settled the financial aspects satisfactorily, Churchill proceeded to sign up his research team,[23] beginning with the young Maurice Ashley.

Faced with a period of history with which he was scarcely familiar, Churchill worked hard and long. As he remarked ruefully, 'The life one leads under the direction of Mr Harrap is the life of one of those prize hens which are kept active by artificial light and pecking at a cabbage leaf always just above its head. One egg being laid, the shell and yolk of the second egg has rapidly to be produced.'[24]

Harrap welcomed his eminent new author with a lavish production. Even the general edition was bound in plum buckram over bevelled boards, while the limited edition (155 sets printed and 150 offered for sale) was slip-cased and bound in sumptuous orange morocco by Sangorski and Sutcliffe. Hand-inserted folding maps and facsimiles were profusely scattered throughout the text.

The first volume was published on 6 October, 1933, and a revised edition appeared in November, 1934, with a further reprint in November, 1939, making a total of 17,000 copies. Fifteen thousand copies of the second volume were printed in two impressions, with an original publication in October, 1934. Two years passed before the third volume appeared on 23 October, 1936, in an edition of 10,000 copies. And again two years elapsed before the publication of the final volume, when 10,000 copies were released on 2 September, 1938.

If at this stage, as in 1898, there was no sign of any distaste on Churchill's part towards the Duke, he had at some time developed a strongly-held antipathy, deriving largely from Macaulay's *History of England*, particularly in the matter of the Camaret Bay letter. Other examples of Macaulay's invective could possibly be dismissed as mere spleen, but the accusation of treason appalled Churchill to the very roots of his being. The crucial passage reads:

'... the secret was much better kept than most of the secrets of that age. Russell, [Admiral Russell, Earl of Orford] till he was ready to weigh anchor, persisted in assuring his Jacobite friends that he knew nothing. His discretion was proof even against all the arts of Marlborough.

Marlborough, however, had other sources of intelligence. To those sources he applied himself; and he at length succeeded in discovering the whole plan of the Government. He instantly wrote to James [II, in exile].'

And of the death of General Tollemache in the Camaret Bay action:

'The public grief and indignation were loudly expressed. The nation...execrated the unknown traitors whose machinations had been fatal to him. There were many conjectures and many rumours....The real criminal was not named; nor, till the archives of the House of Stuart were explored, was it known to the public that Talmash [Tollemache] had perished by the basest of all the hundred villainies of Marlborough.... While the Royal Exchange was in consternation at the disaster of which he was the cause, while many families were clothing themselves in mourning for the brave men of whom he was the murderer, he repaired to Whitehall; and there, doubtless with all that grace, that nobleness, that suavity, under which lay, hidden from all common observers, a seared conscience and a remorseless heart, he professed himself the most devoted, the most loyal, of all the subjects of William and Mary.'[25]

These accusations had haunted Churchill for an indefinable time, and it was not until August, 1924, that a start was made on laying them to rest, during a lunch with Lord Rosebery.

'Lord Rosebery said, "Surely you must write *Duke John* (as he always called him): he was a tremendous fellow." I said that I had from my childhood read everything I came across about him, but that Macaulay's story of the betrayal of the expedition against Brest was an obstacle I could not face. The aged and crippled statesman arose from the luncheon table, and, with great difficulty but with sure knowledge, made his way along the passages of The Durdans to the exact nook in his capacious working library where "Paget's Examen" reposed. "There," he said, taking down this unknown out-of-print masterpiece, "is the answer to Macaulay." '[26]

We must surely treat with some scepticism Churchill's statement that 'from childhood I had read everything I came across about him'. If that was so, why was he prepared to consider Nisbet's offer of 1898 when, as we have seen, he was entirely enthusiastic? And further, Maurice Ashley states in *Churchill as Historian* that 'apart from Macaulay's *History of England* [he] had read comparatively

110

little about the first Duke of Marlborough's life or times'. But, whether or not his antipathy was long-standing, it was certainly emphatic.

'Take this question of the Camaret Bay letter. If John Churchill had written that letter I could not myself have undertaken the writing of this history, and I was deterred from the undertaking because it seemed to me that for a man who held the commission of an officer among soldiers there could be no defence − none that could ever be offered − for writing information that was likely and intended to bring fellow-soldiers into a disastrous ambuscade. Such an action would be indefensible; it would be an offence mortal and immortal, and that is why − although on family grounds I was naturally anxious to rebut such charges − I refrained so long from writing this book.'[27]

Paget's analysis of Macaulay's calumnies − and, more importantly, Churchill's own researches into such archives as the Nairne papers − fired his family pride anew. There were still problems to be faced in Marlborough's less attractive features and actions but, by and large, he could now begin to see his ancestor once again as *sans peur et sans reproche*.[28]

'I hope,' he wrote in the Preface, 'to show that he was not only the foremost of English soldiers, but in the first rank among the statesmen of our history; not only that he was a Titan, for that is not disputed, but that he was a virtuous and benevolent being, eminently serviceable to his age and country, capable of drawing harmony and design from chaos, and one who only needed an earlier and still wider authority to have made a more ordered and a more tolerant civilization for his own time, and to help the future.'

This is going from one extreme to the other with a vengeance, for surely only a process of beatification could accomplish so much. Maurice Ashley's equivalent summary is more human and infinitely more acceptable.

'A first-rate soldier, he was a second-rate statesman. As a politician he was in the main simply an ambitious opportunist who could not bear to be out of office. Excelling chiefly in those diplomatic manoeuvres which could advance himself or his army, he seldom, if ever, exerted his influence for the causes of peace and justice in which he was not directly concerned.'[29]

Clearly the truth must lie in an amalgam of these two views; but that is not my direct concern here. My concern is to examine how and to what extent Churchill chose to present his hero in a refracted light.

Several daunting hurdles faced him when he began to tackle this massive subject. In the first place there were technical problems which forced him to work often at one remove from his sources. His French was weak and his Dutch and German non-existent; he had therefore to rely on translations. It must also be wondered how, with no experience in the period, he even managed to cope with contemporary documents in English; to tackle such calligraphy without knowledge is indeed a path beset by thorns!

In the second place he was largely at the mercy of his devilling assistants when it came to seeking out and evaluating relevant information. In this he was undeniably well served, but such dependence must inevitably have increased the already considerable problems inherent in the process.

It is in this lack of historical expertise that *Marlborough* must first be faulted. It is not, of course, a deliberate slanting on Churchill's part; he simply did not know and therefore an uncontrolled imperfection of vision unavoidably crept in. In a scathing passage in *Churchill: Four Faces and the Man* J.H. Plumb lists a disturbing number of major archives that were either not consulted or, at best, consulted only casually. 'The archival research for these volumes was superficial, exceptionally superficial....The opportunity was there; it was not taken. The biography, huge as it is, remains deficient in its sources.'

Given the evidence, as an experienced politician, Churchill was able to argue closely and accurately. The trouble was not so much that he did not look in the right place for that evidence, it was that he did not always know where the right places were. One must be careful to distinguish, therefore, between interpretative distortions of intent and those of innocence. These deficiencies could only exacerbate the problems that necessarily faced Churchill in studying a period of great political complexity, both nationally and internationally.

It is surely unnecessary to recapitulate the tortuous details of the Camaret Bay letter. To Churchill it was the most important stronghold to attack, and attack it he did, proving to his own complete satisfaction that it was a Jacobite forgery and that the apparently confirmatory note of receipt in James II's *Memoirs* was a later interpolation. His argument is close and impressive, seemingly conclusive, yet even now not all doubts have been stilled; a Scottish court might well bring in a verdict of 'Not proven'. Maurice Ashley (1939) only admits that the letter 'is in all probability a forgery'; while George Malcolm Thomson (1979) says that 'the incident is wrapped in confusion and doubt'. But if Marlborough was indeed guiltless, it is a piquant irony, since double-dealing was so much a central part of his life. There were few occasions when he did not have a careful and cynical foot in either camp. If fabrications were believed, it is hardly anyone's fault but his own.

Churchill, however, was not deterred by uncertainties such as this. He believed that he had achieved a major purpose and had cleared his ancestor of the grave charge of treason. But an objective reading of Marlborough's character and philosophy by no means renders such a charge impossible, and there were other occasions on which it could have been levelled.

By 1686 John Churchill, in company with other leading English nobles, was terminally disillusioned with the reign of James II, regarding the steady erosion of Protestantism and the consequent favouritism towards Catholics as dangerous to the nation and themselves. Accordingly he and they plotted his overthrow.

Now it is very easy to adopt a high moral attitude and insist that Marlborough, as a senior commissioned officer and a leading noble, owed the King — had *sworn* to the King — his total loyalty. It is equally easy to observe that the Civil War and its examples were not *that* distant; it was James's father who was beheaded, after all. Both these statements are true but only partly relevant. It is possibly more relevant that Marlborough's personal future was in danger. As a committed Protestant, he knew that he might be faced in the not-too-distant future with a royal demand that he abjure his religion and embrace Catholicism or face dismissal. In these circumstances it was open to him, of course, to cling to his faith and retire to the country; he could have afforded it easily enough. (Churchill's statement that Marlborough at this time was 'an Earl, but the most impecunious in England' is amusing but scarcely factual.) But wealth and position and power were as vital as breath to Marlborough; as Ashley said, 'he could not bear to be out of office'. Accordingly, he laid his plans and wrote secretly to William of Orange. Apart from his fulsome, and rather pathetic, letter to James on his final separation, he seems to have felt no compunction. Even Churchill, in a strangely enigmatic passage, seems to have recognized this, gloss it though he might.

'How did this prolonged situation, with its many delicate, repugnant, and irreconcilable features, affect his inner mind? Was he distressed or was he indifferent about his personal relations with the King? On the surface he showed no trace of embarrassment. He possessed to a degree almost sublime the prosaic gift of common sense. His sure judgment and serene, dispassionate nature enabled him, amid the most baffling problems of interest and duty, to dwell inwardly and secretly at peace with his gravely taken decisions; and, of course, without further self-questionings to take in due season all measures necessary to render them effectual. The personalities which warm our hearts often cast much away from sentiment or compunction. Not so this man. He made up his mind with cold, humane sagacity, and a profound weighing of all the largest and smallest circumstances; and thenceforward he faced obloquy, if it were inevitable, as calmly as the ordinary chances of battle.'[30]

I have described this passage as 'enigmatic', and so it is. If Churchill intended it as a vindication, his surefootedness has temporarily deserted him, for it is perfectly possible to read it either as defence or attack; the things he says are uncomfortably close to the sort of things that Macaulay said. To present coldness and calculation as desirable, even virtuous, traits is to tread on dangerous ice. And the sentence beginning 'The personalities which warm our hearts' is surely *very* strange. *Do* they, in fact? And what is wrong with sentiment and compunction? Are we being invited to believe that their absence is something worthy?

If this is Churchill's considered defence of a person involved in treason, it is not merely ineffective, it is positively counter-productive. But he does not leave it at that. Some pages later he states categorically (and begging a few questions into the bargain): 'It follows, therefore, that Churchill was right to abandon King James. The only questions open were When? and How? Ought he to have quitted the King when he wrote his first letter of May 1687 to William of Orange? Surely not; the circumstances in question might never have come to pass.'[31]

Well yes, in all honesty, he *should* have quitted the King when he first wrote to William, if he were to maintain any semblance of integrity. To argue that circumstances might or might not have changed is double-edged; it can equally support his clandestine alliance with William or a total relinquishment of any plans for replacing James.

'It was a hideous situation,' Churchill goes on, 'into which he had been drawn by no fault of his own, by no unwise or wrongful action, by no failure of service, by no abandonment of principle.' And that is a farrago of nonsense. The treachery was voluntary and Marlborough played a leading part in it; his betrayal of his loyalty and his commission was both a wrongful action and (specifically) a failure of service, and to do these things without abandoning principle is a moral and ethical impossibility. Churchill is here not merely indulging in special pleading, he is misleading the House; and that is a serious matter.

Without wishing to labour this point overmuch, I would offer one further quotation. 'We need not delve,' wrote Churchill, 'into a painful analysis of Churchill's feelings at this juncture. Lord Wolseley has drawn for us a harrowing picture of the moral and sentimental stresses through which his hero is supposed to have passed on the night of November 23, when he is represented as finally making up his mind to desert James....These well-meant efforts of a friendly biographer have certainly no foundation.'[32]

That they have no foundation, that Marlborough suffered no remorse, no doubts, no pains of conscience, cannot surely be presented as a matter of praiseworthiness; and yet it seems that Churchill is content that it should be so.

Once William was enthroned, Marlborough lost little time in opening secret channels of communication with the exiled James at the Court of St Germains. Initially this was through his nephew, the Jacobite Duke of Berwick. True, the correspondence opened innocently enough, when Berwick wrote to thank his uncle for his kindness to a captured Jacobite; but both saw the usefulness of such a link, and it became an important part of Marlborough's self-concerned diplomacy, as distinct from his more overt policies.

By this means Marlborough carried on his own private peace negotiations with Louis XIV. In his letter to Berwick of 24 August, 1708, and writing under his usual Bond-like 'double-O' cipher, he said: 'I would also assure you that no one in the world wishes for peace with more sincerity than I. But it must be stable and lasting, and in conformity with the interests of my country.' This, if totally lacking in any observance of protocol, is unexceptionable in sentiment; but it must be taken in conjunction with the fact that he had been offered two million *livres* by Louis if peace came about through his influence. Indeed, in his letter of 30 October, he even went so far as to remind Berwick of the *douceur*.

'You may be assured that I shall be wholeheartedly for peace, not doubting that I shall find the goodwill [*ie* the two million *livres*] which

115

was promised me two years ago by the Marquis d'Alègre. If the King and the Duke of Burgundy do not feel that this time is suitable for peace proposals, I beg you to have the friendship and justice to believe that I have no other object than to end speedily a wearisome war.'[33]

One need scarcely point out that it is, to say the least, extremely unconventional for a commander-in-chief to tell his enemy that he is weary of war; such information, broadcast to one's allies, would cause serious alarm and despondency. Matter, indeed, calculated to give comfort to the enemy, and therefore treason. But taken in conjunction with a promised personal fortune, it is a revealing indication of the depth of Marlborough's duplicity, especially as Louis' terms included clauses relating to Spain that were inimical to England, and which he was clearly obliged to support it he was ever to lay hands on the money.

How did Churchill attempt to justify this astonishing liaison?

'It is indeed amazing,' he wrote, 'that any man should have the hardihood to write such a letter to those who regarded him as their most terrible foe – indeed, their only foe. Marlborough is justified before history in pursuing these unauthorised negotiations. In his supreme position, both military and political, he was entitled, on his own judgment and at his own peril, to act for the best for his country, for the Alliance, and for Europe....if he thought it was time to make peace he was right before God and man to do so. But to introduce into this grave and delicate transaction a question of private gain, a personal reward of an enormous sum of money, however related to the standards of those times, was, apart from moral considerations, imprudent in the last degree. Yet this conduct has a palliative feature curiously characteristic of several of Marlborough's most questionable acts. It served interests national, European, and personal at once and equally.'[34]

One must suppose that Churchill was wholly serious in this amazing bit of double-talk. 'Justified before history'? I cannot believe so, given Louis' requirements. 'His supreme position'? But he was a subject of the King, and his military command was shared with Prince Eugen. 'Right before God and man'? Could Churchill really believe that himself, when he immediately uses the phrase 'apart from moral considerations'? If moral considerations are not to be taken into account, what use God – or man, for that matter? And, of course, the last two sentences are the apotheosis of cynicism, and untrue into the bargain.

116

It would be instructive to consider whether Churchill the Prime Minister would have been quite so blithely understanding if (say) Field-Marshal Montgomery had been discovered treating for peace with the Nazis, with a personal fortune thrown in if they were allowed to hang on to Czechoslovakia and Poland. Montgomery would surely have met the same fate as Rommel. And yet, for Churchill the author, Marlborough was right and justified, when in fact he was grossly exceeding his authority, accepting the promise of a massive enemy bribe, and therefore binding himself to support agreements that were certainly not 'in conformity' with the interests of his country.

To quote Churchill's own words about Camaret Bay, 'Such an action would be indefensible; it would be an offence mortal and immortal...'

Finally and briefly, it might be pointed out that Marlborough's last bit of double-dealing was probably his most successful, since his lengthy and entirely self-seeking approaches to the Elector of Hanover during Anne's reign rescued him from ignominy when that person eventually became George I.

Churchill probably made the best of a bad job in attempting to deal with these shameful episodes. He brought to the task eloquence, passion and the powers of a skilful advocate. In these particular cases, however, his best was simply not good enough. A valid point is not negated merely by bluntly stating its opposite, and too often Churchill's zeal led him into just that trap.

One cannot dispute that Blenheim, Ramillies and Oudenarde were great and important victories; Malplaquet was another matter entirely. In his treatment of that appalling battle, Churchill used exaggeration and bias in his attempts to present his hero and his actions in a flattering light.

The battle was, in the first place, unnecessary; in the second, it was foolhardy. To attack such a well-conceived and well-prepared defensive position was far from careful or rational generalship, and the massive Allied losses were only a natural concomitant of arrogant over-confidence. Indeed, to claim it as any sort of victory must be controversial. From the point of view of either side, it could at best be considered a draw. It is true that the French withdrew from the field, but they withdrew in good order and good heart; and they inflicted far heavier losses than they received. Even more importantly, after a series of shattering defeats, they found a new pride, a new confidence; from that moment on, there was no chance of peace — either early or advantageous — whatever Marlborough made himself believe. 'It is now in our power to have what peace we please,' he wrote to Sarah after the battle. But what Malplaquet actually ensured was that peace of any kind was further away than ever before.

Nevertheless, the nation rejoiced, in spite of the fact that powerful contrary voices were quickly raised. Churchill scornfully sets them aside as mere party manoeuvring. 'The Tories thought to represent the battle as a positive disaster. Although the British casualties were under two thousand, they made far more outcry about it than the Dutch, with four times that number.'[35] This astonishing example of chauvinism endeavours to obscure the fact that Marlborough was responsible for the whole Allied army which, in fact, lost one man in every five — 20,000 out of a total of 100,000.

And having vituperatively dismissed a valid criticism about lack of military intelligence by Sir Thomas Mansell[36] as 'curdled venom', he is equally corrosive about the Duke of Argyll's severe, detailed and first-hand accusations of mismanagement and waste of lives. Argyll had been one of Marlborough's commanders at Malplaquet and knew better than any Whig politicians the details of that battle. But the Whigs had the power to howl him down, a tactic that Churchill describes gleefully: 'They celebrated the battle with all the resources and ability of their party and all the machinery of State. The Tories, outmatched by this exuberance, could but look down their noses and mutter insults and calumnies.'[37]

There is no attempt at impartiality here, no attempt at honest analysis of facts and arguments. Anything that smacks of criticism is smeared as 'insults and calumnies'. Churchill hides behind blatant party power-play instead of seeking out the truth and presenting it with an historian's required neutrality. His technique in this matter and elsewhere is merely to make assertive statements, and trust to an air of authority to carry them off; often the passion and exuberance of his language carries the reader on like a surf-rider. But the trouble with surfing is that eventually the collapsing wave deposits the rider high and dry on a motionless shore; and a more rational response is equally deflating to Churchill's approach.

One such example of advocacy by blunt statement is to be found in Churchill's treatment of Marlborough's reactions after the battle. 'The intense strain of the two days' manoeuvre and battle, the long hours at close quarters under the cannonade, the tumult and collision of the cavalry masses, the thirty or forty thousand killed and wounded who cumbered the ground, the awful stake which had been played, left his sober poise undisturbed, his spirit calm.'[38]

If this presents an unintended and chilling portrait of callousness, the picture is reversed within two pages when Churchill hastily tries to set matters right. 'Upon no one was the impression of the slaughter more deeply marked than upon Marlborough. It disturbed his mind; it affected his health; it changed his sense of values.'[39]

Thus the statement, but one looks in vain for evidence. Having stated that 'considering all the rough work he had to do, he was astonishingly sensitive,' all Churchill offers are two quotations of stunning banality. ' "It is melancholy," he [Marlborough] wrote, "to see so many brave men killed, with whom I have lived these last eight years, when we thought ourselves sure of a peace." He was unmanned by the plight of the wounded, of whom at least fifteen thousand of all nations and both armies were left upon his hands. "I have hardly had time to sleep, being tormented by the several nations for care to be taken of their wounded." '[40] If to be unmanned is merely to complain petulantly about a temporary shortage of sleep, Marlborough was unmanned; no other evidence is offered.

Unlike the other battles, where he could and did adduce supporting material to back up his arguments, Churchill is here reduced to what is little more than bluster; and it does not convince.

I have so far considered some areas of major historical importance in which Churchill has presented a case rather than evaluated dispassionately; where he has been defending counsel rather than judge. These areas, I believe, support my contention that in *Marlborough* he cast a sideways light on his subject with the firm intention of restoring Marlborough's glory unblemished by a single flaw, and he fought his corner with a less-than-punctilious regard for strict truth. To put it more bluntly, this was not a matter of historical inexperience; this was deliberate distortion. As with the earlier biography, as with all his books, he was presenting *his* case, pleading *his* cause.

Even with the more trivial facts of Marlborough's life, Churchill refused to relax. His language remains slanted, his arguments one-sided. Let us take the unquestionable fact of Marlborough's monumental avarice and meanness. Examples abound: Marlborough borrowing sixpence for a sedan chair and then walking home; the delightful suggestion that he left his i's undotted in letters to save ink; his extreme reluctance to entertain his officers. There are too many such stories, and even the most apocryphal are merely additional testimony to the fact.

Churchill spends much time in endeavouring not to rebut, since

119

that was always a forlorn hope, but to minimize and justify this aspect of Marlborough's character. Marlborough was brought up in poverty, and the fear of returning to that state made him, even as a millionaire, even more tight-fisted than the notorious Oofy Prosser. Alternatively, he was wealthy and powerful, but it was only by managing his wealth with the utmost self-sacrificial rigour that he could be sure of maintaining that position. Alternatively again, such parsimony was a positive Christian virtue.

It is accepted that Marlborough laid the foundations of his fortune by taking out an annuity with Lord Halifax with part of the £5000 he received from his mistress Barbara Villiers. For a down-payment of £4500 he obtained an annual sum of £500 for life. Macaulay, as might be expected, was caustic: 'He was thrifty in his very vices, and levied ample contributions on ladies enriched by the spoils of more liberal lovers.' Not to put too fine a point on it, the young John Churchill was, in modern terms, a gigolo. His amours were both notorious and profitable.

But what did Churchill have to say about this gift from Barbara Villiers? 'The code of the seventeenth century,' he wrote, 'did not regard a man's taking money from a rich mistress as necessarily an offence against honour.' An extraordinary statement, that, and there is no supporting authority offered. But in what century is a man who does such a thing not regarded as anything other than a kept man? In his early days, Marlborough *was* a kept man, and a very willingly kept man; that, surely, is the long and short of it. John Churchill – page and ensign – used his physical attractions and virility to good and intentional effect.

Churchill takes many pages in his attempt to neutralize this well-documented calculation, most of them in attacks on Macaulay, in which he quotes a succession of Macaulay's epigrammatical criticisms in the apparent belief that they will be automatically and universally rejected. But the approach, this time, is self-defeating. For who could honestly disagree with Macaulay's statement that 'All the precious gifts which nature had lavished upon him he valued chiefly for what they would fetch.' Marlborough's continual seeking after ever-higher rewards justifies the remark in full. And then again, who can really take offence at Macaulay's other neatly-balanced and accurate judgment: 'At twenty he made money out of his beauty and his vigour; at sixty he made money out of his genius and glory.' Snide maybe, but undeniably and elegantly valid.

Marlborough is huge – over a million words and more than five times Churchill's initial proposed length – heavily documented, comprehensive. No future historian can hope to avoid indebtedness, and no unprofessional reader can fail to be moved by the grandeur of the vision, the language and the myth. Sonority piles on sonority, vista succeeds vista, magnificence follows magnificence.

Yet simple flaws gnaw at the foundation. In his Preface, Churchill set himself an impossible task. He postulated a giant among men, a paragon of all virtues, a model for mankind. But he ignored, in his familial zeal, the fact that Marlborough was just a human being, had virtues, faults, contradictions just as other, lower mortals do. He was far more complex than Churchill allowed and, in paradox, far simpler, far more a man of his coldly calculating and cynical age than Churchill could admit.

Marlborough remains a major historical work for all its faults. Although he failed to use many relevant archives, Churchill mopped up so many, and used them so freely, that no one now can hope to supersede his work. There have already been – and, one hopes, will continue to be – more balanced portrayals of Marlborough, but it would be a bold author and an even more generous publisher who could venture to take on another investigation in such depth.

Once again he presented a case as he would in Parliament, and once again he emerged from the arena on the winning side. He had deliberately set out to make a demi-god of Marlborough ('a Titan') and, for the general reader, he succeeded in presenting the image he required.

It is, however, crucial and salutory to recall his revealing words to Maurice Ashley: 'Give me the facts, and I will twist them the way I want to suit my argument.'[41]

In both his biographies Churchill carried out this precept to the letter. Both were written as exercises in familial justification. Both are presented in the guise of a restored truth, yet neither merits the claim on examination. They must remain major biographies, but they do not really earn the description. Churchill acquired both commissions through family influence, and they both bear unmistakable marks of his homage to that influence.

Let me finish with deep irony. Paget, in his biting analysis of Macaulay, wrote, 'The attention of the reader is excited, his sympathies are awakened, his passions are aroused; he devours page after page and volume after volume with an appetite similar to that which attends upon the perusal of the most stirring fiction; he closes the book with regret, and then, and not until then, comes the reflection that he has been listening to the impassioned harangue of the advocate, not to the calm summing-up of the judge.'[42]

A magnificently apt description of Churchill's *Marlborough*. But it is Macaulay himself, in a passage on Herodotus, who unwittingly provides the final verdict: 'He has written an incomparable book. He has written something better, perhaps, than the best history; but he has not written a good history.'[43]

It is, perhaps, an anticlimax to descend from the high complexities of *Lord Randolph Churchill* and *Marlborough* to the breezy simplicities of *My Early Life* and *Great Contemporaries*. Neither is overtly contentious, neither seeks to make more than gentle points, though an occasional barb can still be felt. These, together with *Thoughts and Adventures*, represent the lighter end of Churchill's output and, as such, need not delay us too long.

My Early Life appeared on 20 October, 1930, and by the end of the year had sold more than 11,000 copies. Since then many translations, cheap and paperback editions and the film *Young Winston* have made it easily the most popular and widely read of all Churchill's books. Other books have had massively higher initial sales, such as *The Second World War*, but this is not at all the same thing. Indeed, a strong case could be made out for awarding *The Second World War* the title of the least-read best-seller in publishing history. In the case of *My Early Life* the popularity is deserved, for it is, quite simply, a gem.

The autobiographical Churchill is a mellow Churchill, sitting back comfortably after dinner with brandy and cigar and reminiscing about far-off days. In spite of the alarms and dangers of his early years, he is more concerned here with extracting humour from a given situation than with recounting it as it was at the time.

But if this is an unbuttoned Churchill, it is also in some ways a masked Churchill; there is a deceptive blandness, a rosy impressionistic haze over his backward glance. Many events are over-simplified, others have their sting safely drawn. By way of a small example, he states that he wrote *Savrola* in two months. As we have seen, nothing could be further from the truth, for it was written over a three-year period. But then he always deprecated the novel, which, he said, 'I have consistently urged my friends to abstain from reading'.

Of somewhat greater importance is the way in which he has toned down the horrors. The carnage of Omdurman, though delineated excitingly enough, is drastically played down compared to the bloody and vivid immediacy of his *Morning Post* letters; and Kitchener's shade is left in peace. Similarly, it is the high adventure of the Boer War that is emphasized rather than those things which moved him at the time; the inept High Command, the expensively outmoded strategy and tactics, the often-needless human waste. And as we have already seen (Chapter II) he treats his first experience of being under fire very differently indeed.

My Early Life stands alone in the Churchill canon, an essentially lightweight but sunny delight; it seems impossible to believe anything other than that it virtually wrote itself. The pace is so infectious, the development so swift and economical, the style so naturally engaging that it is difficult to imagine the author struggling with revisions. He must have enjoyed writing this book, and it shows on every page.

But there was surely still a purpose behind it, apart from the obvious one of making money. Written amid the settling dust of his 1929 resignation, it served to keep him before the public in spite of his lower political profile; and certainly it was intended to reassure the public that, whatever his opponents or the Press might have been saying about him, he really was − *honestly* − a good bloke.

Although concerned with other men's lives, *Great Contemporaries* cannot in any way be compared to *Lord Randolph Churchill* or *Marlborough*. Its genesis was in the columns of popular magazines and newspapers rather than in the research library, and in this respect it must be grouped with *Thoughts and Adventures*.

During the period 1931-1936 Churchill wrote a succession of profiles of some of his eminent contemporaries, the majority of whom were personally known to him, though only two − T.E. Lawrence and F.E. Smith, 1st Earl of Birkenhead − could be described as close friends. The articles appeared initially in various publications ranging from *Nash's Pall Mall* and *Strand* on the one hand to the *Daily Mail* and *News of the World* on the other. They were therefore avowedly written for a middle- or lower-middlebrow audience and are consequently little more than general summaries. Churchill was never interested in muck-raking or, indeed, even in deeply analytical investigation. Given his preferences and the limiting requirements of the media involved, it is therefore unrealistic to expect anything controversial; these are by no means profiles in the *New Yorker* sense. And he was rarely a grudge-bearing man; he could see and write of the best even in people who had treated him shabbily; in this respect, Asquith and Balfour escaped lightly indeed.

Even Hitler was treated with circumspection. He had only been in power for two years, and Churchill was waiting to see how he would develop. While he was openly critical of Hitler's policies towards the Jews, left-wingers and trades unionists, he could still write: 'the world lives on in hopes that the worst is over, and that we may yet live to see Hitler a gentler figure in a happier age.'

Nevertheless, as the chapter on his journalism demonstrated, even this mildness led to official protests.

Considering his restraint of his language about Hitler, it is perhaps surprising that there was no protest about his essay on Trotsky, which he called, with unusual malice and not a little touch of anti-semitism, 'Trotsky, *alias* Bronstein.' 'He must have been a difficult man to please. He did not like the Czar, so he murdered him and his family. He did not like the Imperial Government, so he blew it up. He did not like the Liberalism of Guchkov and Miliukov, so he overthrew them. He could not endure the Social Revolutionary moderation of Kerensky and Savinkov, so he seized their places. And when at last the Communist régime for which he had striven with might and main was established throughout the whole of Russia, when the Dictatorship of the Proletariat was supreme, when the New Order of Society had passed from visions into reality, when the hateful culture and traditions of the individualist period had been eradicated, when the Secret Police had become the servants of the Third International, when in a word his Utopia had been achieved, he was still discontented.'

While this acid summary apparently raised no protest at the time, it is interesting to note that Churchill himself took steps to censor his words for a wartime reprint of *Great Contemporaries*. By that time (1943) relations with Russia were already becoming difficult, and he gave instructions that both the essay on Trotsky and − for different reasons − that on Roosevelt should be dropped. It is, however, a little difficult to see why he should have worried about insulting Trotsky (and therefore Stalin?) at that juncture.

But for the most part *Great Contemporaries* shows the author in a benign mood, just as *Thoughts and Adventures* is largely a relaxed book, with only one or two prophetic clouds to mar the sunniness. Both his temperament and the editorial requirements tended to draw any stings that might otherwise have been present. And, of course, there was the consideration that several of his subjects were still alive: men like George Bernard Shaw, the deposed King Alfonso XIII of Spain, Baden-Powell and Roosevelt. But if his approach had limitations, whether externally or internally imposed, he was still capable of frequently lighting the character with flashes of personal insight, often coupled with dramatically heightened language, as in this passage from his study of T.E. Lawrence.

'The world feels, not without a certain apprehension, that here is someone outside its jurisdiction; someone before whom its allurements may be spread in vain; someone strangely enfranchised, untamed, untrammelled by convention, moving independently of the ordinary currents of human action; a being readily capable of violent revolt or supreme sacrifice, a man, solitary, austere, to whom existence is no more than a duty, yet a duty to be faithfully discharged. He was indeed a dweller upon the mountain tops where the air is cold, crisp and rarefied, and where the view on clear days commands all the Kingdoms of the world and the glory of them.'

Passages like this illuminate the subject, if perhaps impressionistically, with a sudden flare of colour — the dramatic emphasis of the stage spotlight. They recur with gratifying frequency throughout the book.

'Hindenburg! The name itself is massive. It harmonizes with the tall thick-set personage with beetling brows, strong features and heavy jowl, familiar to the modern world. It is a face that could magnify tenfold, a hundredfold, a thousandfold, and it would gain in dignity, nay, even in majesty; a face most impressive when gigantic.'

'Fancy paints nations in symbolic animals — the British Lion, the American Eagle, the Russian double-headed ditto, the Gallic Cock. But the Old Tiger, with his quaint, stylish cap, his white moustache and burning eye, would make a truer mascot for France than any barnyard fowl.' (Of Clemenceau.)

'Few people practise what they preach, and no one less so than Mr Bernard Shaw....No one has ever led a more respectable life or been a stronger seceder from his own subversive imagination. He derides the marriage vow and even at times the sentiment of love itself; yet no one is more happily or wisely married. He indulges in all the liberties of an irresponsible Chatterbox, babbling gloriously from dawn to dusk, and at the same time advocates the abolition of Parliamentary institutions and the setting up of an Iron Dictatorship, of which he would probably be the first victim.'

Great Contemporaries, though only in the second rank of Churchill's books, is one of his most amusing and enjoyable. It is

125

also, in spite of its limitations, a useful source of information and impressions of some of the leading figures of those years, and incidentally sheds much light on the author himself. The essays 'may be what journalists called "angled"; the light, admittedly, passes through a most powerful prism, which serves both to stain its radiance and deflect its direction. Even so, there is a richness in their texture, a glow about them, even though only reflected from their creator's own zest for living.'[44]

Great Contemporaries was first published on 4 October, 1937, and a revised edition containing four extra profiles appeared on 7 November, 1938. Of the first edition, a total of 15,000 copies was printed, while the revised edition consisted of 5000 copies, followed – unexpectedly, perhaps – by a reprint of 28,000 in August, 1939.

VIII

THE HISTORIES

BUT *was* Churchill an historian? He was certainly a politician, a war correspondent, a biographer, a novelist, an essayist, a painter, a bricklayer even; but was he — and did he thoroughly *wish* to be — an historian?

In the face of fifteen volumes of historical works, the question may seem obtuse; he clearly wrote histories and popular opinion considers him a great writer in that field. Professional opinion, however, is rather more cautious; even allowing for the understandable distrust of the academic for the commercially successful amateur (or at least semi-professional), there seem to be good reasons for doubting that Churchill was ever truly an historian.

It is surely the task of the historian — and here I tread like Agag — to consider, analyse and assess with scrupulous objectivity. An historian may not grind axes, though, one is forced to admit, occasional examples can be found.

Churchill, however, never met the basic requirement, never made any attempt to do so, and never wished to do so. Whatever he wrote was written with a specific aim in view. Whether that aim was personal advancement, the propounding of a political creed or the rehabilitation of a discredited forebear, he wrote from a position that was well off-centre. Sometimes he made no secret of his stance, as in *Marlborough*, but frequently he endeavoured to camouflage his position, with varying degrees of success.

Churchill's three histories have been consistently attacked by academic historians on two fronts: their inaccuracy in some details, and their overall lack of objectivity. The former is relatively unimportant; the latter is surely a matter of exquisite irony, for in both his accounts of the wars, he went out of his way to deny that quality, to emphasize the purely personal nature of his narratives.

If, in these two works, he was overt in his stance, he was more covert regarding the motives behind *A History of the English-Speaking Peoples*. In the earlier works he was concerned to explain — and, to an extent, to justify — past events and decisions with which he had been intimately concerned. In his last, he had a hidden cause: the strengthening of the historic ties between Britain and America, in preparation for the struggle with Germany that he knew was inevitable. It was conceived and commenced in the early Thirties, but the original motivation happily — if that is the *mot juste* — translated, in the postwar era, into the terms of the Cold War.

Of all Churchill's works, *The World Crisis* was intended, first and foremost, as a personal apologia. Although the second and final report of the Dardanelles Commission, published in November, 1919, did not in any way blame him for the failure of that well-conceived but lamentably executed campaign, he had endured many attacks; and the publication of the report stirred up new controversies. He therefore felt compelled to defend himself, not only against the past, but also for the future. As he later wrote to Bonar Law (3 March, 1923), 'It is only by publishing certain documents and telegrams which I have written myself and for which I bear the prime responsibility, that I can deal with the lies and fictions which have ruled for so long and which I have borne all these years without making any reply, while every other version has been put before the public.'

Initially he visualized only a two-volume work dealing with his performance as First Lord of the Admiralty, and the finality of the closing pages of Volume II confirms this intention. It seems clear, then, that these first two volumes should be considered as virtually separate from the rest of the work, both in intention and structure. They carry the story only from 1911 to the evacuation of the Dardanelles in 1915, the point at which Churchill's involvement as First Lord ceased.

So, stung into retaliation, he began to dictate his story and, at the same time, commissioned Macmillan (the publisher of *Lord Randolph Churchill*, his last substantial work) to set up in type his official minutes and memoranda.

In November, 1920, he appointed Curtis Brown as his literary agent, giving them a free hand provided that they earned him a minimum of £20,000. For the first volume, Thornton Butterworth offered an advance of £9000 plus £2500 for American rights, but these terms were subsequently improved to the extent that Scribner doubled the American offer, and the sale of serialization rights added a further £13,000 from *The Times* and the American magazine *Cosmopolitan*. Churchill thus had well over his £20,000 from the beginning.

His agreement with Thornton Butterworth was, however, startling, possibly even unique, in that it specified a royalty of 33⅓%. In a letter to his wife, Churchill happily worked out the arithmetic.

'The book is to be published at 31/6. Deduct one-third, equals 10/6, trade commission, leaves 21/-. Deduct 1/- for distributing agencies, leaves 20/-. Deduct one-third of the original published price, equals 10/6, my share, leaves 19/6, out of which he [Thornton Butterworth] has to supply the paper, the ink, the binding, the maps, the advertising and his own profit. On top of this he has to pay me £9000 before he secures a penny...,When 10,000 of each volume have been sold, he will have got clear of the £9000 he pays me in advance. On every volume sold after that I get another 10/6.'[1]

Seven thousand three hundred and eighty copies of Volume I appeared on 10 April, 1923, following serialization in *The Times* and elsewhere. Volume II (7500 copies) was published on 30 October, 1923, with reprints totalling over 14,000.

In view of the fact that the action of these two volumes was laid on both land and sea, Churchill originally proposed the title of *The Great Amphibian*[2]; perhaps fortunately, Scribner rejected this and insisted on *The World Crisis*, a title both more euphonious and more suited to the final structure of the work.

Although Churchill intended these volumes primarily as self-justification, he was at pains to emphasize the accuracy of his narrative and his honesty in dealing with the documentation. Truth, in other words, would be his shield.

'... I feel it both my right and my duty to set forth the manner in which I endeavoured to discharge my share in these hazardous responsibilities. In doing so I have adhered to certain strict rules. I have made no important statement of fact relating to naval operations or Admiralty business, on which I do not possess unimpeachable documentary proof. I have made or implied no criticism of any decision or action taken or neglected by others, unless I can prove that I had expressed the same opinion in writing *before the event*.'[3]

And he went on, regarding his publication of official documents,

'... lest it should be thought that there have been any material suppressions, or that what is published does not truly represent what occurred, or the way things were done, I affirm my own willingness to see every document of Admiralty administration for which I am responsible made public provided it is presented in its fair context.'[4]

Claimed objectivity apart, these are surely fighting words under the urbane surface. In the first three sentences there is certainly the subtle suggestion that others have not been so scrupulous. The following sentence warns the reader that there will no absence of criticism, and the final statement of willingness to see publication of the documents cannot be interpreted in any other way than a challenge.

In Volume I, therefore, Churchill laid out his wares as an honest trader; Volume II − covering a period in which, significantly, he came closer to major criticism than in the preceding book − took the matter a little further. In a period (1911-1914) during which his actions as First Lord were both far-sighted and courageous, objectivity was satisfactory. Faced in the succeeding volume with the fiasco of the Dardanelles, perhaps a little more distancing was required.

'I must...at the outset disclaim the position of the historian. It is not for me with my record and special point of view to pronounce a final conclusion. That must be left to others and to other times. But I intend to set forth what I believe to be fair and true; and I present it as a contribution to history of which note should be taken together with other accounts.'[5]

Clearly Churchill thought that he had made his position sufficiently clear, but in this he was mistaken. There were misinterpretations enough, of which Balfour's, perhaps predictably, is one of the most crass: 'Winston has written six volumes of autobiography and called them history.'[6] But if we actually read Churchill's words as he intended them to be read, with what reaction do we come away?

In the first place − and this is the more heavily reinforced the further we get into *The World Crisis* − we come away with a renewed recognition of his burning hatred of war.

'All the horrors of all the ages were brought together, and not only armies but whole populations were thrust into the midst of them....

Germany having let Hell loose kept well in the van of terror, but she was followed step by step by the desperate and ultimately avenging nations she had assailed. Every outrage against humanity or international law was repaid by reprisals often on a greater scale and of longer duration. ...The wounded died between the lines: the dead mouldered into the soil. Merchant ships and neutral ships and hospital ships were sunk on the seas and all on board left to their fate, or killed as they swam. Every effort was made to starve whole nations into submission without regard for age or sex. Cities and monuments were smashed by artillery. Bombs from the air were cast down indiscriminately. Poison gas in many forms stifled or seared the soldiers. Liquid fire was projected upon their bodies. Men fell from the air in flames, or were smothered, often slowly, in the dark recesses of the sea....When all was over, Torture and Cannibalism were the only two expedients that the civilized, scientific, Christian States had been able to deny themselves; and these were of doubtful utility.'[7]

This is writing — and feeling — that vividly recalls his outrage after Omdurman, and the leopard's spots were now even more indelibly imprinted, for after Omdurman he had written, 'There is no worse extravagance in war than an economy of soldiers'. Less than twenty years later, and having personally tasted the mass destruction of the First World War, his views had become less coldly strategic and more those of the poor bloody infantry.

'As in the shades of a November evening, I for the first time led a platoon of Grenadiers across the sopping fields... the conviction came into my mind with absolute assurance that the simple soldiers and their regimental officers, armed with their cause, would by their virtues in the end retrieve the mistakes and ignorances of Staffs and Cabinets, of Admirals, Generals and politicians — including, no doubt, many of my own.'[8]

This is, in itself, a significant change of view, and an understandable one; but it is only a sidelight. What is more revealing is the way in which Churchill, overtly seeking to defend himself against attack, handled the explosive subject of the Dardanelles. He had nothing to fear in his handling of the Admiralty up to the point when his conception of the campaign began to crumble through a mixture of pusillanimous strategical assessment and faint-hearted political leadership. It was the Dardanelles campaign specifically that had prompted him to arm himself and come out fighting. One might therefore expect his treatment of it to be full-blooded.

Surprisingly, it is actually muted; still, in fact, claiming objectivity.

'...it is my intention to set forth the facts as they are known to me concealing no essential.'[9]

In hindsight it seems indeed as if Churchill felt himself to be armoured in truth. His narrative is almost withdrawn, as well it might be, faced with that appalling carnage: it is as if he is holding himself back. Only at a few points do his feelings break out; at, for instance, the appointment of General Monro to replace Sir Ian Hamilton.

'He belonged to that school whose supreme conception of Great War strategy was "killing Germans". Anything that killed Germans was right. Anything that did not kill Germans was useless, even if it made other people kill them, and kill more of them, or terminated their power to kill us.... General Monro was an officer of swift decision. He came, he saw, he capitulated.'[10]

But this was virtually his only spurt of anger – though perhaps 'contempt' would be a better word. And surely it was justifiable, for if any one man destroyed the Dardanelles campaign it was Monro. The military buck might have stopped at Kitchener, but that was merely a matter of protocol. In the circumstances Churchill displayed remarkable stoicism in the face of his shattered dreams.

But his summing up of the campaign is both aware of the problems and bitter at the surrender to them.

'...we see Cabinet and Admiralty able to face the first alternative [evacuation] and shrink from the second [Admiral Keyes' plan to force the Dardanelles]. While time is young, while prospects are favourable, while prizes inestimable may be gained, caution, hesitancy, half measures rule and fetter action. The grim afternoon of adverse struggle alone brings the hour of desperate resolve. The hopeful positive is rejected while all may be gained; the awful negative is embraced when nought but escape remains in view; and the energy and conviction which might have commanded victory are lavished upon the mere processes of flight.'[11]

One can see clearly enough why Churchill was so often out of favour! The years since 1916 had been a long and bitter struggle against his own political colleagues and, in spite of his endeavours to the contrary, some of his frustrations spilled over, even though they were only expressed in general terms. And the frustrations were only aggravated during the writing by the fact that he was no longer even a Member of Parliament.

The next two volumes[12] can conveniently be considered together. For much of the period covered by them Churchill was away from the centre of government, and when he returned, his post as Minister of Munitions was not of the first rank. Nevertheless, he continued to adopt his personalised viewpoint and again tried to make this clear to his audience. 'I try to present the reader at once with a comprehensive view of the mighty panorama and with a selection of its dominating features; but I also tell my own story and survey the scene from my own subordinate though responsible station.'[13]

And again, writing of Daniel Defoe's *Memoirs of a Cavalier*: 'In this delightful work the author hangs the chronicle and discussion of great military and political events upon the thread of the personal experiences of an individual. I was immensely encouraged to find that I had been unconsciously following with halting steps the example of so great a master of narrative.'[14] But in spite of all these endeavours, he was under no illusion this time that he had succeeded in hammering the point home. Even as late as 1930, in the Preface to the one-volume, abridged edition, he still felt it necessary to return to it.

> 'It is a contribution to history strung upon a fairly strong thread of personal reminiscence. It does not pretend to be a comprehensive record; but it aims at helping to disentangle from an immense amount of material the crucial issues and cardinal decisions.'

In spite of all this, many military readers remained hostile, as they had been when faced with the early war despatches; and some historians, notably J.H. Plumb, were scathing. 'A very uneven book,' he wrote, '...largely story-telling, eschewing analysis in depth and devoid of penetrating studies of personality'; but he admitted that it was, if handled with care, 'an invaluable source for that age'.[15]

However, there were more generous judgments, particularly by J.M. Keynes. Reviewing Volume III in *Nation and Athenaeum*, he wrote that Churchill 'pursues no vendetta, and shows no malice...a tractate against war − more effective than the work of a pacifist would be'. And later, in *New Republic*, he went further, showing himself to be wholly cognisant of Churchill's intentions and attitudes.

'With what feelings does one lay down Mr Churchill's two-thousandth page? Gratitude to one who can write with so much eloquence and feeling of things which are part of the lives of all of us of the war generation, but which he saw and knew much closer and clearer. Admiration for his energies of mind and his intense absorption of intellectual interest and elemental emotion in what is for the moment the matter in hand − which is his best quality. A little envy, perhaps, for his undoubting conviction that frontiers, races, patriotisms, even wars if need be are ultimate verities for mankind, which lends for him a kind of dignity and even nobility to events which for others are only a nightmare interlude, to be permanently avoided.'

The volumes contain some of Churchill's finest writing, illuminated and inspired still by his detestation of modern warfare. Certainly he delighted *as a writer* in the hugeness of the canvas, weaving the many threads together with majestic ease, touching in the details with brilliant colours, describing the massive battles in terms which fitly combine relish of the literary challenge with an awareness of the sombre tragedy of the events. Here he is, for instance, on the Battle of the Somme.

'The anatomy of the battles of Verdun and the Somme was the same. A battlefield had been selected. Around this battlefield walls were built − double, triple, quadruple − of enormous cannon. Behind these railways were constructed to feed them, and mountains of shells were built up. All this was the work of months. Thus the battlefield was completely encircled by thousands of guns of all sizes, and a wide oval space prepared in their midst. Through this awful arena all the divisions of each army, battered ceaselessly by the enveloping artillery, were made to pass in succession, as if they were the teeth of interlocking cog-wheels grinding each other.

'For month after month the ceaseless cannonade continued at its utmost intensity, and month after month the gallant divisions of heroic human beings were torn to pieces in this terrible rotation. Then came the winter, pouring down rain from the sky to clog the feet of men, and drawing veils of mist before the hawk-eyes of their artillery. The arena, as used to happen in the Coliseum in those miniature Roman days, was flooded with water. A vast sea of ensanguined mud, churned by thousands of vehicles, by hundreds of thousands of men and millions of shells, replaced the blasted dust. Still the struggle continued. Still the remorseless wheel revolved. Still the auditorium of artillery roared. At last the legs of men could no longer move: they wallowed and floundered helplessly in the slime.'[16]

As might be expected, the set pieces — Verdun, the Somme, the Marne — are magnificently structured and brilliantly delineated. As at Omdurman and Spion Kop, Churchill's broadly sweeping vision was at its best in his flowing descriptions of mighty battles — an aspect of his talent that also appeared to superb advantage in *Marlborough*.

Volume III appeared in two simultaneous parts over three years after its predecessor, on 3 March, 1927. Just over 7500 sets were published and reprints virtually doubled that figure. The author received an advance of £2000 against a royalty of 30%.

Volume IV, subtitled *The Aftermath*, appeared in an edition of 7500 copies on 7 March, 1929, with reprints totalling a further 3500. There was an advance of £2500 against a similar royalty.

At this point, Churchill believed that the task was completed, and *The Aftermath* was a broad retrospection in which his anti-war feelings rose to fresh peaks of abhorrence and bitterness. He found also a voice to prophesy. The prophecies went unheeded and came to pass.

'It is probable — nay, certain — that among the means which will next time be at their disposal will be agencies and processes of destruction wholesale, unlimited, and perhaps, once launched, uncontrollable.

'Mankind has never been in this position before. Without having improved appreciably in virtue or enjoying wiser guidance, it has got into its hands for the first time the tools by which it can unfailingly accomplish its own extermination. That is the point in human destinies to which all the glories and toils of men have at last led them. They would do well to pause and ponder upon their new responsibilities. Death stands at attention, obedient, expectant, ready to serve, ready to shear away the peoples *en masse*; ready, if called upon, to pulverize, without hope of repair, what is left of civilization. He awaits only the word of command. He awaits it from a frail, bewildered being, long his victim, now — for one occasion only — his Master.'[17]

And faced with the repellent but inescapable image of future war, he wrote bitterly and sadly.

'It has at least been stripped of glitter and glamour. No more may Alexander, Caesar and Napoleon lead armies to victory, ride their horses on the field of battle sharing the perils of their soldiers and deciding the fate of empires by the resolves and gestures of a few intense hours. For the future they will sit surrounded by clerks in offices, as safe, as quiet and as dreary as Government departments, while the fighting men in scores of thousands are slaughtered or stifled over the telephone by machinery. We have seen the last of the great Commanders. Perhaps they were extinct before Armageddon began. Next time the competition may be to kill women and children, and the civil population generally, and victory will give herself in sorry nuptials to the spectacled hero who organises it on the largest scale.'[18]

Characteristically, his closing words were a clear warning, in which he pinpointed the twin perils still looming before an exhausted Europe.

'The task is not done. The greatest exertion must continue to be made over a long period of years. The danger of war has by no means passed from the world. Old antagonisms are sleeping, and the drum-beat of new antagonisms is already heard. The anxieties of France and Germany are only partly removed....Russia, self-outcast, sharpens her bayonets in her Arctic night, and mechanically proclaims through self-starved lips her philosophy of hatred and death.'[19]

Considered as Churchill intended it to be considered, *The World Crisis* is clearly one of his most brilliant works; indeed, Robert Rhodes James claims it as his greatest. As he never tired of reiterating, it was not history nor ever intended to be, but a personal narrative and a personal justification. As he had written to his wife on 29 December, 1921, 'It is a gt chance to put my whole case in an agreeable form to an attentive audience.'

The final volume, *The Eastern Front*, appeared on 2 November, 1931, in an edition of approximately 5000 copies. It had not been originally visualised, and was not a labour of love − except to the extent that it gave Churchill more ever-needed income. Maurice Ashley is quite blunt: 'I received the impression that [it] was written primarily to earn money.'[20] Certainly it was not written with the first-hand experience that shaped and imbued the first four volumes; and some of the ground had already been covered therein. Nevertheless it is an intermittently vivid account of the political and military complexities of the titanic struggle that culminated in the Revolution of 1917. But, as Lloyd George wrote in his *War Memoirs* (1933-34), 'Mr Churchill's morbid detestation of the Revolution that in 1919 baffled his most ingenious military dispositions has rendered him incapable of weighing fairly the causes that led to the downfall of autocracy.' But of course Churchill had little interest, when faced with the 'Red Menace', in 'weighing fairly'. The book is, typically, political advocacy mixed with some superb set-piece descriptions of the major battles. Ashley is perhaps overkind in his judgment that '...it is right to regard this swiftly written book of Churchill's not merely as an extremely useful and informative essay on military and political history but also as a significant sidelight thrown upon his own career and attitudes as a statesman in time of war.' I agree that the book is valuable for its expression of Churchill's views, and for the magnificence of the battle scenes, but I would also regard it as a relatively minor work written, as Ashley says, primarily for money.

If this was indeed the main motive, then the sales performance must have gratified the author. True, it sold fewer than its predecessors — under 8000 copies — but it earned Churchill about £4000 in all by its royalty of 30% and advance of £2500.

Whatever can be said of the preparation and production of *The World Crisis* can also be said of *The Second World War*, but several times more strongly. The same research and writing techniques were used, the same personal viewpoint adopted, the same meticulous and apparently never-ending revision insisted upon. But everything was that much larger. It was not merely that the task itself was immense, so also was the purely physical struggle to write it against a background of political decline and repeated illnesses. Lord Moran's analysis is illuminating on this point.

'Five of the six volumes of *The Second World War* were...written when Winston was still in opposition. If, however, the dates at the end of each preface are set beside the dates of his four strokes or cerebral storms it will be seen that the book was written under difficulties.

'They are as follows:

March 1948	Vol. I *The Gathering Storm*
January 1949	Vol. II *Their Finest Hour*
August 1949 Stroke at Monte Carlo	

January 1950	Vol. III *The Grand Alliance*
February 1950 Disturbance of cerebral circulation	
September 1950	Vol. IV *The Hinge of Fate*
September 1951	Vol. V *Closing the Ring*
July 1952 Stroke	
June 1953 Stroke	
September 1953	Vol. VI *Triumph and Tragedy.*[21]

Churchill started work on the war memoirs in 1946, collating information and even writing before any arrangements were made regarding publication, and turning first of all to Lord Ismay for help and advice. Almost immediately information and documents began to flow in, including the private diaries of (*inter alia*) Lord Alanbrooke, Sir Stafford Cripps, Alfred Duff Cooper, Lord Moran and Jock Colville.[22] At the same time, he formally sought government approval of his intention to publish official documents.

It was not long, however, before satisfactory financial arrangements were made. Time-Life offered $1,150,000 for the American serialization rights alone, while Houghton Mifflin proposed $250,000 for the book rights. Information regarding the arrangements with Cassell have not been released, but the amount of money involved can perhaps be judged by the fact that the directors had to sell a considerable number of shares to raise it. So began the construction of what has been described as 'one of the great monuments of British publishing'. The complexity of the ensuing operation is such that it cannot be dealt with here; full details will be found in Appendix II.

At this time, Churchill visualized the book as being in five volumes; however, as the atmosphere of the Cold War hardened, he became increasingly worried that he might be blamed for the postwar confrontation with Russia. Accordingly he proposed a sixth volume as an act of self-justification, a proposal that was strongly opposed by Cassell and by Lord Camrose, who had bought the British serialization rights. Stubbornly, he rejected their advice and wrote *Triumph and Tragedy*, a volume that is, in its own way, as sad and unnecessary as the volumes of postwar speeches.

In 1946, of course, that was all in the future. Heavily defeated in the election, he found life as Leader of the Opposition unbearably frustrating. 'I feel I could do things,' he complained to Moran. So the researchers and the experts were assembled once more, led by F.W. Deakin. Inevitably, it was a lengthy and laborious task, and the first volume took almost three years to appear.

As can be seen from the figures quoted below, the print-runs of
The Second World War were unprecedented. The British and
American first impressions can best be tabulated.

	British	American
The Gathering Storm	221,000	75,000
Their Finest Hour	276,000	35,000[23]
The Grand Alliance	300,000	61,000
The Hinge of Fate	275,000	70,000
Closing the Ring	275,000	60,000
Triumph and Tragedy	200,000	60,000

The work was serialized pre-publication both in the *Daily
Telegraph*(for a reputed fee of 'very much over £50,000') and the
New York Times; and these appearances, together with the books
themselves, brought in many thousands of corrections and revisions,
all of which were examined in detail and adopted if proved correct.
Foreign editions abounded, and included French, German
(Germany and Switzerland), Belgian, Danish, Norwegian, Dutch,
Swedish, Finnish, Italian, Spanish, Portuguese, Hebrew,
Argentinian, Brazilian and Japanese. The first two or three volumes
were also translated into Greek, Turkish and Russian (the last
published in America.)

As with *The World Crisis,* Churchill set out to write a personal
view of events, not a formal history. Even during the war he realized,
alone among the leading statesmen involved, that he might one day
write of the war, and he amassed and even arranged material as he
went along.[24] The eventual appendices, consisting of hundreds of
documents, vividly demonstrate the remarkable range of his interests
and provide a unique picture of a war-leader at work. But their
publication carried its own pitfall: a built-in irresistible temptation
on the part of readers to regard the work as definitive history. In *The
World Crisis* the documents quoted traced his wartime career – from
the Admiralty to the Ministry of Munitions – and they are thus more
readily acceptable as one man's view of events. But, with *The Second
World War*, the very fact that he was Prime Minister automatically
gave the work an authority and a weightiness that tended to obscure
the fact that it *still* presented only one man's view. Once again he
issued a disclaimer: the work was not history but a 'contribution to
history'. Again he referred to Defoe's *Memoirs of a Cavalier*, using
a wording almost identical to that used in *The World Crisis*. The
gesture was as futile as it had been before.

It is not my task here to endeavour to assess the validity of his views. It is sufficient, perhaps, to observe that *The Second World War* is, in its way, as much an individual report as is, say, in *its* way, *The River War*.

There is, however, one essential difference. The early campaign books and *The World Crisis* — even to an extent, *Marlborough* — were all very much books of their time. By the second half of the Forties, though, the world had moved on into an exhausted flatness that had little to do with, and little time for, the high-flown attitudes and language of Churchillian rhetoric. During the war, under the press of events, and because it was starkly necessary for survival, the people had responded to the emotion, the grandiloquence, the rolling exhortations and the snarled defiance. They responded not merely to a call to patriotism but to a call for awareness of the destiny of the British people as Churchill saw it — that almost mystical concept of international duty that pervaded all of his life. The war years were exalted, heady years; when the dangers were past, normality and anticlimax asserted themselves.

In that period of reaction, his words and style were often too flamboyant. To be sure, *The Second World War* broke all existing sales records apart from those of *The Bible*, but that does not necessarily mean that the style and attitudes were as much a reflection of their day as were those of his earlier books. I have commented earlier, *à propos* his Boer War despatches, that his language could often be aversive to modern readers, and this is certainly true of a significant proportion of *The Second World War*. It was, of course, dictated and, as a result, is often verbose and overblown. As Maurice Ashley observed, 'Good books do not necessarily need to be long books. But books are almost bound to be long if they are dictated by an orator.'[25] What, for instance, is the younger reader to make of the following passage?

'We may, I am sure, rate this tremendous year as the most splendid, as it was the most deadly, year in our long English and British story. It was a great, quaintly-organised England that had destroyed the Spanish Armada. A strong flame of conviction and resolve carried us through the twenty-five years' conflict which William III and Marlborough waged against Louis XIV. There was a famous period with Chatham. There was the long struggle against Napoleon, in which our survival was secured through the domination of the seas by the British Navy under the classic leadership of Nelson and his associates. A million Britons died in the First World War. But nothing surpasses 1940. By the end of that year this small and ancient Island, with its devoted Commonwealth, Dominions and attachments under every sky, had proved itself capable of bearing the whole impact and weight of world destiny. We had not flinched or wavered. We had not failed. The soul of the British people and race had proved invincible. The citadel of the Commonwealth and Empire could not be stormed. Alone, but upborne by every generous heart-beat of mankind, we had defied the tyrant in the height of his triumph.'[26]

One can, perhaps, forgive Churchill the beating drums and the waving banners. Regardless of his political rejection by the people, he wanted – *needed* – to continue to inspire the country, to continue to mould it to fulfil again the British destiny. He remained unswervingly constant to his beliefs, the last survivor of the great Whig tradition and probably the last exponent of the chivalric code;[27] but the people moved away in their own direction. In 1946 he had wanted to call the first volume of his new work *The Downward Path*; the title could be applied, with bitter irony, to the period in which he wrote.

One other difference can be noted between the early campaign books and *The Second World War*: there is present in the latter a pervasive spirit of charity that is noticeably lacking in certain aspects of the earlier books. Churchill's 'Moral' of the work itself supplies that quality, and it is interesting that this 'Moral' was composed word for word as early as the first half of the Twenties.

'When the Great War was over, he produced one day a lapidary epigram on the spirit proper to a great nation on war and peace. "In war, resolution; in defeat, defiance; in victory, magnanimity; in peace, goodwill." (I wish the tones in which he spoke this could have been recorded – the first phrase a rattle of musketry, the second "grating harsh thunder", the third a ray of sun through storm-clouds; the last, pure benediction.)'[28]

This new-found benevolence is a further reason why *The Second World War* cannot be taken as objective history, quite apart from its author's stated intentions. It led to reticences that obscured the actual details of wartime difficulties, particularly in the sphere of personalities. Later and less restrained writers than Churchill have adopted more forthright attitudes, but such was not his wish. The battle was over, forgiveness and goodwill were to be the order of the day – even, on the surface, to de Gaulle.

Nevertheless, the work is even now commonly referred to as his 'war history'. As I have tried to demonstrate, it is overtly, undeniably, only one man's version. It is, it might almost be said, an unfortunate coincidence that its author happened also to be one of the victorious leaders. Provided it is taken as prescribed, however, the work is — and always will be — a unique source for all future students. For once, Professor Plumb summarizes the position positively: 'Churchill the historian lies at the very heart of all historiography of the Second World War, and will always remain there. And the book will continue to be read....It is, in spite of its theme — war and destruction — a heartening book.'[29]

Just so. And the book is heartening largely because of the author's insistence on the continuing tradition and mythos of the British people, in which that terrifying war is viewed by Churchill as one more glorious link in a predestined and unbroken chain. While it was important to him to tell his own story, it was surely even more important — and of more lasting importance — to put forward yet again his passionate faith in Britain's destiny.

But he had not quite finished. On 5 February, 1959, 25,000 copies of an abridged, one-volume edition appeared, edited by one of his assistants, Denis Kelly. It contained a specially-written Epilogue in which he looked back at the years 1945 to 1957.

In an otherwise bland overview, he returned yet again to the theme of a united Europe. Quoting his own words from a speech at Zurich University (19 September, 1946), and in a striking reflection of his position after the First World War, he made the following exhortation.

> 'Germany must be deprived of the power to rearm and make another aggressive war. But when all this has been done, as it will be done, as it is being done, there must be an end to retribution. There must be what Mr Gladstone many years ago called "a blessed act of oblivion"....The first step in the re-creation of the European family must be a partnership between France and Germany....There can be no revival of Europe without a spiritually great France and a spiritually great Germany.'[30]

And he went on, again in words which echoed his warning at the end of *The World Crisis*:

> 'But I give you a warning. Time may be short. At present there is a breathing space. The cannon have ceased firing. The fighting has stopped; but the dangers have not stopped. If we are to form the

142

United States of Europe or whatever name or form it may take, we must begin now.'[31]

Finally, turning away from Germany to consider the problem of Russia, he offered his view of the future in words that are a quite remarkable prevision of some aspects of the situation that Russia is now facing. As with Nazi Germany during the Thirties, once he had warned, he offered understanding and hope.

'Russia is becoming a great commercial country. Her people experience every day in growing vigour those complications and palliatives of human life that will render the schemes of Karl Marx more out of date and smaller in relation to world problems than they have ever been before. The natural forces are working with greater freedom and greater opportunity to fertilise and vary the thoughts and the power of individual men and women. They are far bigger and more pliant in the vast structure of a mighty empire than could ever have been conceived by Marx in his hovel....human society will grow in many forms not comprehended by a party machine. As long therefore as the free world holds together, and especially Britain and the United States, and maintains its strength, Russia will find that Peace and Plenty have more to offer than exterminatory war. The broadening of thought is a process which required momentum by seeking Opportunity-for-All who claim it. And it may well be if, wisdom and patience are practised that Opportunity-for-All will conquer the minds and restrain the passions of Mankind.' [32]

In December, 1932, Churchill agreed with Cassell that he would write *A History of the English-Speaking Peoples* for the outright sum of £20,000 for publication rights. He was still deeply engaged in the early stages of *Marlborough*, and for most of the Thirties he worked simultaneously on these two major undertakings.[33]

He did not, however, begin active work on the history until the autumn of 1934, when he engaged Keith Feiling as an adviser.

'As you know, I wish to give special prominence in the first section of the work to the origin and growth of those institutions, laws and customs and national characteristics which are the common inheritance, or supposed to be, of the English-speaking world. Language and literature play a large part, and indeed these studies would be as it were threaded together by a vivid narrative picking up the dramatic and dominant episodes and by no means undertaking a complete account.' [34]

143

He went on: 'There is of course no question of research of any kind, but of course we should base ourselves wherever possible upon the original sources.'

During the next few months, Feiling produced fourteen draft chapters, at which point he pleaded pressure of work and was replaced by F.W. Deakin.

From the letter just quoted, it is immediately apparent that Churchill was now taking his 'writing by committee' to extremes. No longer were his advisers merely expected to devil; they had to produce coherent narratives upon which Churchill would work and on which he would impress his own style and personality.

Marlborough took up a majority of his time during the mid-Thirties, and it was not until 12 August, 1938, that he sent the first instalment to Cassell, consisting of the first chapter and part of the second. In that year, however, the last volume of the biography was completed and henceforward he was able to concentrate on the history.

More advisers appeared on the scene or rejoined the team. Alan Bullock was commissioned to prepare a 10,000-word summary of the early history of Australia and New Zealand, while Maurice Ashley agreed to write similar amounts on the Stuarts and Cromwell. Churchill wrote to him on 24 March, 1939:

> 'In the main, the theme is emerging of the growth of freedom and law, of the rights of the individual, of the subordination of the State to the fundamental and moral conceptions of an ever-comprehending community. Of these ideas the English-speaking peoples were the authors, then the trustees, and must now become the champions. Thus I condemn tyranny in whatever guise and from whatever quarter it presents itself. All this of course has a current application.'

Conveniently and perhaps appropriately, Churchill completed this first text on the day that war was declared, when he delivered to Cassell approximately half a million words.

In 1945 he turned first to the task of writing his war memoirs, and only in 1953 did he begin to reconsider the earlier work. Alan Hodge was called in to read the text and report on what had to be done, but, in spite of his view that the problems were not serious, Churchill did nothing until his retirement in 1955, when he finally returned to the proofs.[35]

This time, in deference to his age and health, he was determined to do things the easy way. 'I've been living on *The Second World*

War,' he said to Lord Moran. 'Now I shall live on this history. I shall lay an egg a year — a volume every twelve months should not mean much work.'[36] As a consequence, his advisory panel was larger than ever before, and was entirely comprised of leading professional historians; no more were there any promising youngsters like the Ashleys and Deakins of former years. Before the war three advisers (Feiling, Deakin and G.M. Young) had sufficed; after the war the team included Alan Hodge, A.R. Myers, Joel Hurstfield, D.S. Pennington, A.L. Rowse, J.H. Plumb, Steven Watson, Asa Briggs, Maurice Shock and, as specifically American advisers, Frank Feidel and M.A. Jones.

Work proceeded steadily, and certainly tranquilly compared to the complexities of *The Second World War*.[37]

The first edition of Volume I, consisting of 130,000 copies, was published on St George's Day, 23 April, 1956, on which day Churchill also laid the foundation stone of Cassell's new offices. A second impression of 30,000 was rushed through in the following month, with further reprints over the next ten years totalling nearly 65,000.

Volume II appeared on 26 November, 1956, Volume III on 14 October, 1957, and Volume IV on 14 March, 1958; each consisted of 150,000 copies.

Public and academic opinion was adulatory, but perhaps the best comment came from Churchill's grandson Winston, who wrote on 14 May, 1957, to say, 'It is so much easier reading than the history books we read at school and your vivid description brings it all to life.' And the doyen of historians, G.M. Trevelyan, wrote that the time would come 'when they will stop reading us professional historians but not you'.[38]

Any assessment of *A History of the English-Speaking Peoples* must take two factors into account: firstly, the greatly increased level of contribution from the advisers; and secondly, Churchill's age and ill-health.

The fact that he was now being presented with draft texts inevitably limited his own room for manoeuvre, and therefore the scale of his personal contributions. Gone were the days — or rather the nights — of striding up and down the room dictating to relays of secretaries and an admiring audience of hired experts. Now he was much more alone in his reworking. In *Churchill: Four Faces and the Man*, J.H. Plumb states that 'Churchill was too old, too tired to undertake the detailed work necessary to bring himself up to date with the previous forty years of English historical scholarship.... His greatest pleasure, which Lord Moran also reveals, as he worked over the proofs, was to savour the sentences, to change an epithet here and there, or reverse the order of phrases, break up sentences and sharpen them... detailed application was too burdensome for him. He was too old, too tired.'

Now, too, he no longer had the energy to argue with his staff. In *Churchill as Historian*, Maurice Ashley commented that his experts 'largely succeeded in muffling his exuberance', but, at the same time, he complained of the lack of Churchillian 'asides'. There are indeed few of his characteristically epigrammatic descriptions and judgments, and virtually no virtuoso set-pieces such as had added so much to the flavour of his earlier major works. To an extent, of course, this can be ascribed to the fact that he had to cover a lot of ground; there was simply no room for passages of high-flown rhetoric. But I suspect that in earlier days Churchill would have overcome this limitation. Age was indeed taking its toll.

In these pages it has incidentally become clear, I think, that Professor Plumb is a somewhat hostile witness, in spite of his flattering reviews published during Churchill's lifetime. Nevertheless, his judgment of *A History of the English-Speaking Peoples*, though harshly expressed, is more defensible than some of his others. 'In those fields where his work challenges comparison with professional history, Churchill remains, at the most generous assessment, a gifted amateur. His abilities are clear − narrative power, grasp of structure, and a rich, full-blown style. His weaknesses are equally glaring − paucity of historical knowledge, lack of analytical power, and an ignorance of economic, social, and intellectual history of staggering proportions. The major significance of these works will lie in the fact that Churchill was the author. They illuminate his mind far more than they do the subjects he wrote about.'[39]

Leaving aside the fact that Churchill constantly reiterated that he was *not* writing history, the value of this judgement lies in the last sentence. His books *were* personal statements − self-revelations − from the beginning, and Plumb has fairly consistently fallen into the familiar trap of ignoring Churchill's own clear words.

His intentions in writing *A History of the English-Speaking Peoples* were made utterly plain in the Preface to Volume I: 'This book does not seek to rival the work of professional historians. It aims rather to present a personal view on the processes whereby

English-speaking peoples throughout the world have achieved their distinctive position and character.'[40]

Beyond this desire, of course, lay the ulterior motive. In this case, Churchill wished to create a work that would strengthen the ties between Britain and the rest of the English-speaking world, in particular, between Britain and the United States. He had believed for a long time that another war with Germany was inescapable, a knowledge only made more certain by the advent of Adolf Hitler. He sought, therefore, to persuade the Americans out of their isolationism to take their part in the resistance to the Nazi threat.

By the time the book was published, however, that threat had been eliminated, and the West faced another one, which, again, Churchill had long foreseen.

'If there was a need for it [the history] before, that has certainly not passed away. For the second time in this present century the British Empire and the United States have stood together facing the perils of war on the largest scale known among men, and since the cannon have ceased to fire and the bombs to burst we have become more conscious of our common duty to the human race. Language, law, and the processes by which we have come into being, already afforded a unique foundation for drawing together and portraying a concerted task. I thought when I began [in the Thirties] that such a unity might well notably influence the destiny of the world. Certainly I do not feel that the need for this has diminished in any way in the twenty years that have passed... On the contrary, the theme of the work has grown in strength and human thought is broadened.'[41]

And at the end, as in other, earlier, works, he insisted on warning his readers that the fight is not yet over, and that they must still 'go forward, till the whole task is done'.

'Here is set out a long story of the English-Speaking Peoples. They are now to become Allies in terrible but victorious wars. And that is not the end. Another phase looms before us, in which Alliance will once more be tested and in which its formidable virtues may be to preserve Peace and Freedom. The future is unknown, but the past should give us hope.'[42]

In that last sentence lies the crystallization of Churchill's central belief that history, and especially British history, is both a guide and an inspiration. More than that, British history held for him the force of myth; it is a view, perhaps, of some naïveté and oversimplification, but if it is a view that sustained and fortified him through long adversity, then it is also a view of validity and power.

> '...it is from that very history that we may derive strength and wisdom which we need so sorely now. This is the day [Empire Day] to remember the Sovereigns, heroes, warriors and statesmen who brought it through the grim centuries of the past.
>
> 'Let us think of Queen Elizabeth and her bold sea-captains curbing the might of Spain, and keeping the horrors of the Inquisition from our shores. Let us think of Oliver Cromwell, John Hampden, and the founders of our Parliamentary government. Today our eyes may follow the long red columns of Marlborough's army marching from the North Sea to the Danube to change the history of Europe and save it from becoming a fief of Louis XIV. Today we may live with Clive before Plassy, and with Wolfe dropping down the St Lawrence to scale the Heights of Abraham. Once again we see the inspiring image of the greater Pitt bidding "with flashing eye and outstretched arm England to be of good cheer". Once again we may see the Iron Duke amid the battle-smoke of Waterloo lay the might and splendour of Napoleon in the dust.'[43]

Rattling good stuff, that; rousing and romantic. It is also an extremely good illustration of Churchill's inspirational view of history. Implicit in it also is his unswerving vision of Britain's past as a moulding and preparation for world leadership, and for him that leadership was not domination and power, but responsibility, the fulfilment of a sacred duty. 'It is this union of past and present, of tradition and progress, this golden chain, never yet broken, because no undue strain is placed upon it, that has constituted the peculiar merit and sovereign quality of English national life.'[44]

For reasons already discussed, *A History of the English-Speaking Peoples* is a lot more sober than those last two extracts, but the same spirit, the same immoveable national faith, imbue every chapter. In my Introduction I described it as a 'bravura swan-song'. Bravura it certainly is, in the context of advanced age and ill-health; in stylistic terms it is perhaps a muted swan-song. But as a framework for his passionate and enduring belief in this country's future — upborne always by its past — it is a worthy swan-song; and one of which, with all respect to Professor Plumb, many professional historians might well be proud.

IX

SUMMARY

In the preceding pages I have examined in some detail the way in which Churchill wrote every single one of his books with an ulterior motive, far removed from the simple joys of authorship. I have considered the ways in which those books either advanced him politically or established (to his own satisfaction, at least) a thesis that was important to him. Into these considerations I have drawn such matters as public and academic opinion, sales and earnings. It is now time to endeavour to create a compound from all these elements, and reach general conclusions.

It is not from mere cowardice that I claim that this is not easy. It is never simple to sit in judgment on a man as Protean, and who has stirred so many passionate and conflicting opinions, as Churchill.

We can start, however, with the indisputable fact that he was an enormously successful writer. His earnings, from as early as 1899, were astonishing, particularly when adjusted to contemporary monetary values.[1]

Further, the fact that for decades publishers continued to offer him high advances is clear indication that such investments were fruitful. An examination of print figures, taken in conjunction with reprint figures and dates, shows that Churchill consistently gave his publishers value for money; in the period following the Second World War individual first print-run levels of up to 300,000 suggest very considerable value indeed. And what is more, the continual existence of substantial reprints proves that he gave equal value to the public.

In the sphere of journalism also, the fees were impressive, and editors were ever eager to include his name among their contributors.

All this is unarguable, but it merely establishes that he was popular and commercially successful, nothing more. What it does not do is offer any guide as to whether he was a *great* author, since commercial success does not necessarily equate with quality.

The immediate question, therefore, is whether the scale of these earnings sprang from a recognition of literary excellence, or whether it resulted more from his political eminence. Initially, certainly, it was his writing that gained respect during the period 1897-1900, but in later years, once he had established a political reputation, it seems clear that his words and ideas were so consistently and rewardingly published at least partly because it was Churchill the politician who was propounding them, a proposition supported by the fact that editors were happy to publish articles by him of such triviality that, written by a mere X or Y, they would have been rejected – and certainly never commissioned.[2]

Clearly, then, his extra-literary reputation is an inescapable factor in both his commercial success and his literary reputation. Adulation is, by its very nature, all-embracing and uncritical, and even now that reputation is still significantly enhanced by the memory of his years as war leader.

There was also, of course, the snowball effect. His books had sold well from the very first, so that the longer he went on, the more he could approach a publisher or editor not only as a leading public figure but also as an author with a proven and continuing track record.

However, it was not his reputation as writer that *primarily* concerned Churchill (except insofar as it created wealth); to him the priority was that he wanted to win the contest of the moment. Whether that contest was the rehabilitation of Marlborough or the castigation of the government's air force development policy, the defusing of Hitler or the establishment of himself as a celebrity, the fight, not the creation of literature *per se,* was the thing. These factors must remain clearly in view if any accurate judgement is to be reached.

In Chapter IV I touched briefly upon the question of whether collections of speeches should properly be considered in an examination of a writer, since, by a strict definition, they are not *written.* I concluded that they should. The question, however, insists on re-appearing, for how can a man who dictated even his 'written' works be considered a writer? There are, of course, other examples (Edgar Wallace is perhaps the best-known) and the question can once again be put firmly in its place.

Nevertheless, the question does raise a very important stylistic matter. When Edgar Wallace, a very experienced journalist, used dictation, his words eventually appeared on the printed page as a reflection of his journalism. But when Churchill, a politician and orator, used the same method of composition, his words appeared as — what?

And in this contrast lies the seed of both his popular reputation as a great writer, great historian, great biographer, and of much of the academic distrust with which he has been met. For his literary style is unavoidably heightened, embellished, even on occasions blatantly overblown. Reginald Pound hit this particular nail very accurately.

'His only use for a pen was to correct and interpolate. One was constantly aware of his voice. Adjectives were flying buttresses of the argument. Without them his vocabulary would have been fairly commonplace.'[3]

I have already quoted, in Chapter VIII, a thoroughly orotund passage from *Their Finest Hour* as a vivid example of the faults that dictation can inflict upon a writer, especially one whose earliest models were Gibbon and Macaulay. Such passages abound in Churchill's books and, as I have already observed, are largely responsible for his popular reputation. (Another, incidentally, is the sheer length to which he wrote, for surely only great authors can write long books!) But these faults must seriously weaken any assertion that he was a great writer or a great stylist. He was always a powerful writer, an exciting writer, a persuasive writer, even a moving writer. But I must doubt that he was, overall, a great writer, even though there are many passages of fine writing in his books; the trouble is that so often these passages are Fine Writing rather than fine writing.

He used his voice to write because he was accustomed to use it in his work as a politician, and this is another example of his subordination of literary to non-literary considerations. The technique offered advantages, however; his rolling phrases, his remorseless rhythms, his thunderous adjectives, frequently did much to carry his points. And, for Churchill, the points came first.

Each book was intended to do a specific job of work, a job chosen with firm intention. Each was planned and written with that end in view. The subordinations, therefore, were neither casual nor accidental; they were deliberate. And as a direct result of these subordinations, he surrendered the possibility of being considered a great historian and biographer.

But, paradoxically, *and directly because of those same subordinations,* he came to write books that were, in Macaulay's phrase, 'something better, perhaps, than the best history', for those very imbalances gave him the wherewithal to write two biographies and three histories that possess more immediacy, more vividness, more sheer impact than many that are more correct and experienced. The academic judgments are right; but the popular view, in its own way, is also right, for Churchill — ironically, in view of his sometime detestation — became the twentieth-century Macaulay, with all Macaulay's towering gifts of language, all his obliquity and partiality, all his fallibility. But, mercifully, without his spleen.

Yet if it is ironic, it is also superbly fitting that they should share the same gifts and faults as historians. Both grind their axes with formidable certainty, both carry their points with breath-taking use of language, both speak vividly to the common reader. To neither does one look for a balanced portrayal, to neither does one look for objectivity. One seeks instead, and finds, majestic English, wide-ranging vision, and a continuing and passionate belief in the greatness of their country.

But which, I wonder, as they lie down together, is the lion and which the lamb?

It is always dangerous, sometimes even fatal, to make assumptions or to ascribe possible reactions to others. Yet I think it might be justifiable to *suspect* that Churchill himself would not have been displeased with my description of him as a literary gladiator. He was a fighter from the beginning – ever a fighter – and his writings, which reflect that quality so truly, are among the most important manifestations of his long, awe-inspiring and multi-stranded life.

CHURCHILL'S METHOD OF WRITING

LORD Randolph Churchill was the first and last major work that Churchill tackled single-handedly; it was also the last he physically wrote. From then on, he employed variable teams of research assistants and specialist advisers, and dictated the initial drafts. The system has been described as 'writing by committee', but in fact it was a lot less democratic than that phrase suggests.

In the first place, the members of the team were required to feed him with raw material. This involved devilling, commenting, summarising, suggesting. Books were bought for the library if possible, but on occasion Churchill would demand just the relevant pages — a piece of vandalism that shocked more than one helper.

Secondly, the assistants were required 'to make sympathetic and co-operative noises while Churchill dictated' (Maurice Ashley's description). Once he had started he preferred to keep a full head of steam, and his staff were expected to sit and supply facts on demand. Criticism of the main line of argument was not, at that stage, at all welcome.

(It is interesting to note at this point Churchill's need for the feeling of speedy progress, even if it was illusory. He loved to explore, to draft, to get things down on paper, no matter that the result might be scrapped next morning. Ashley has recounted how he was astonished by Churchill's dictating an introductory chapter to *Marlborough* 'before, as far as I could make out, he knew anything at all about him beyond the skeleton of his career as it was familiar to every schoolboy'.)

Thirdly, the team was required to answer specific queries, and frequently these were complex and abstruse. In a letter to Keith Feiling dated 18 July, 1932, Churchill wrote: 'I am anxious to set my story to the early life of Marlborough upon a true background, especially in the reigns of Charles II and James II. I was specially interested in your view that there is much more to be said for the foreign and naval policy and financial administration of Charles II than we were taught at school.[1] I should like to dignify this part of English history and the men who made it as far as possible. For this purpose what I want is not a mass of detail, but only true, broad, general facts and a clear chain of causation. Why did these different wars occur? What were the forces operating on the national and royal minds? What were the main stresses which were the good or foolish plans etc. etc. Some vignettes of the principal figures eg. Bennet, afterwards Arlington, who was the patron of Winston Churchill. Was the cabal so thoroughly disreputable as we have been led to believe? Both Charles II and Louis XIV became their own Prime Ministers in this period. Did they do better or worse than those who had preceded this change?'

All of which would probably have furnished an entire book in its own right! And if on that occasion he required 'only true, broad general facts,' this was not always the case. Of another adviser, Lt-Commander Owen, for instance, he demanded deeper digging:

'There are however two points upon which I should be much obliged if you can help me. The first you mentioned yourself about Marlborough being the only Cabinet Minister who did not volunteer to take command of the fleet after Torrington's defeat at Beachy Head. I have not come across this in any detail in my own readings. Perhaps you could give me the reference of the passage itself. Is there any record of the orders issued to Talmash for the Brest Expedition? Was he, for instance, told to attack Brest only if he found it unprepared, or was he to attack anyhow? Was he given any discretion about attacking other places if Brest was found to be too strong? There were presumably sealed orders for the expedition.'[2]

Surrounded by his attentive team, then, Churchill would dictate into the small hours, striding up and down the room while a relay of secretaries took his words down in shorthand. Typescripts were presented to him on the following morning for revision or rejection.

Quite apart from this relentless nocturnal activity, Churchill's days were also crammed. His related correspondence was always vast. During 1933, when working on the early stages of *Marlborough*, for instance, 'he received 62 letters from Maurice Ashley, 16 from Keith Feiling, 30 from Colonel Pakenham-Walsh, and 15 from Professor G.M. Trevelyan. In addition, on technical matters connected with the printing of the chapters, he received 154 letters from C.C. Wood[3] and 12 from George Harrap. Churchill himself wrote 80 letters to Ashley, 51 to Wood, 12 to Feiling, 17 to Pakenham-Walsh and 8 to Trevelyan. Churchill's complete *Marlborough* correspondence for 1933 alone contained 420 letters that he received, and 308 which he wrote.'[4]

And, of course, while all these historical and technical matters were being dealt with, there was also at Churchill's elbow his indefatigable Private Secretary Edward Marsh, who acted as arbiter on style and punctuation. Having joined him at the Colonial Office in 1906, he was still deeply involved in the preparation of Churchill's books when he died in 1953. Just how involved he was, and respected were his opinions, can be judged from the following letter from Churchill, sent on 16 May, 1933, with the first batch of *Marlborough* proofs. The original text is lengthy and demanding, but even in the following edited form the degree of reliance that Churchill placed on Marsh is clearly visible.

'I now send you twenty-seven of the twenty-nine or thirty chapters of the first volume of *Marlborough*....These form a complete narrative and have already undergone two or three revisions....The points I want you particularly to mark are:
1. Clumsy sentences where the meaning is obscure or the grammar questionable.
2. Repetition of words. I have a good many favourites and they may crop up too often, e.g., vast, bleak, immense, formidable etc...
4. Repetitions of arguments...

5. Dull, boring, stodgy passages...
6. Cheap, vulgar, undignified references...
7. Hyphens... capitals and punctuation throughout...'[5]

And so on. This detailed list of demands was a considerable compliment to Marsh, who rose to the challenge with typically donnish fastidiousness. Churchill told Ashley that a proof read by Marsh was 'an education in itself', and wrote to Marsh to say that he was 'delighted with the way you have increased in some instances the precision, in others the euphony of a sentence.'

Once a section of typescript was ready to proceed to the next stage, it was sent direct to a printer (usually the Chiswick Press) for setting and proofing in wide galley form. As Churchill admitted, he found it easier to work on a printed page (wouldn't we all!) and could afford to pay for the privilege, claiming to Ashley that he recovered half the cost from the Inland Revenue. He was also quite ruthless in his approach to the proofs. As he wrote to George Harrap on 18 July, 1932, during his work on the first volume of *Marlborough*:

'The great advantage of working on these large galley proofs is that one sees practically three pages of typescript at a glance. This enables the structure to be much more easily shaped. You must not however suppose that I attach any finality to the proofs, because they are printed. I always knock them about a great deal and incorporate the criticisms of any authorities who may read them....I am only expecting you to give me the usual allowance for author's corrections, namely £50 for each volume. The rest of the expense for proof corrections I bear myself, though I rely on you to get the best terms from the printers.'

Revise would follow revise, eventually to become a 'Final Revise'; this title, however, rarely fulfilled its promise. More often than not 'Overtake Corrections' then began to arrive, sometimes even after the presses had started running. In the case of *The Second World War*, this complex process resulted in a situation whereby Volumes II and IV had, respectively, two and three complete and variant texts.

This method of composition continued up to the end, with the added development, when Churchill returned after the war to *A History of the English-Speaking Peoples*, that assistants were frequently asked to provide draft chapters. These were, however, *only* drafts, to be treated in any way Churchill saw fit. Predictably, some experts retired hurt by his handling of their contributions. Ashley, however, could apparently relish the fate of one of his.

'I was once invited to write a draft chapter about Oliver Cromwell, for which I was handsomely paid. Years afterwards, when Churchill's second volume appeared, I turned idly to it to find out what he had, in fact, written about Cromwell and the Interregnum. I was astonished to find some of my facts and phrases embedded in it, but the whole draft had been stood completely on its head.'[6]

As that comment shows, Churchill sought to control the contents of his books to the end, at least in the sense that he continued to rework and personalize, but to a noticeably diminishing degree, the draft material submitted by his assistants.

THE SECOND WORLD WAR:
PUBLISHING AND PRINTING HISTORY[1]

As a practical example of the complexities caused by Churchill's writing methods, discussed in the previous Appendix, it is enlightening to consider in some detail the publishing and printing history of *The Second World War*.

The equivalent of the typescript, as far as publishers were concerned, took the form of galley slips, seventy sets of which were printed for Churchill by the Chiswick Press, for his use in seeking comments from expert advisers and in disposing of subsidiary rights. These galleys were set to normal page-width, complete with most of the preliminary matter, and decorated with three-line dropped capitals of Old Face Open, though they were not broken up into pages. Each volume included textual variations, to such an extent that Volume II had two complete versions and Volume IV had three. In some cases (*eg* Volume IV) a printing strike necessitated the mimeographing of certain parts of the text.

One can picture easily enough the disturbed mixture of relief and despair with which editors and production managers must have greeted the arrival of the first set. On the one hand, it contained the statement that this was the 'Final Text', while, on the other, there was the ominous reservation of full freedom of proof correction. In any event, any feeling of foreboding would have been fully justified, for the work turned into what must have been a production nightmare.

This text was followed a little later by the 'Revised Final Text', also in the same galley form, which completely superseded all previous versions. Many chapters were almost completely rewritten and pages were transposed.

Even after this corrections continued to flow in. (As late as 1955, for the 'Chartwell' illustrated edition, Churchill was still correcting and polishing.) In his history of *The House of Cassell* (Cassell, 1958), Simon Nowell-Smith described the process at work, when the author began to receive letters of correction after the serializations in the *Daily Telegraph*, the *New York Times* and elsewhere, all of which were scrupulously investigated and adopted if proved reliable. 'Cassell's received anything up to twenty-five lists of corrections and alterations to their text which had to be incorporated before the author was satisfied that he had his best.'

On the other side of the Atlantic, too, similar complications developed. A further idea of the scope and persistence of the process can be gained from the statement made by the Houghton Mifflin Company in the catalogue to the Benjamin Franklin-Winston Churchill Exhibition at the University of Pennsylvania in 1951. According to them, it began with the arrival of copy in the form of galleys with the author's corrections added. This went for typesetting, and then the 'Revised Final Text' arrived, marked to conform with

American usage. This, in its turn, went for typesetting. Proofs eventually went back to the author, who cabled (!) his corrections back. Page proofs were then submitted and checked, and final make-ready work was commenced. Churchill continued to send what he called 'Overtake Corrections' which were still arriving after the electroplates had been made, and a number of pages had to be replated. And finally, further directions began to arrive concerning revisions to be made in the second printing.

As time went by, Houghton Mifflin, understandably enough from their point of view, refused to accept any more corrections and ran the first impression. Although their action resulted in their securing overall priority (not to mention scooping the Scandinavian market), it also resulted in their edition being sadly deficient. To take but two superficial points, it lacked all the folding maps present in the Cassell edition, and the maps in the text are printed in one colour only, against two- or even three-colour printings by Cassell who, by patient persistence, included all the stipulated corrections.

The first volume appeared in America on 2 June, 1948, followed at a distance by the British edition on 4 October, 1948.

The reasons for American precedence are not to be found only in the matter of corrections, however, for British economic conditions provided hazards unknown in the United States.

'Its production had to be planned and put into operation while paper rationing was still in force. The company's paper supply, bearing in mind other commitments, was obviously totally inadequate and a generous allowance was granted from the Moberley Pool – the special reserve held at the disposal of a committee of publishers for essential works. As soon as the company's representatives began to canvass orders for the first volume, however, it quickly became apparent that even these supplies would be quite inadequate. At their wits' end the directors took the only other step open to them: they reduced the size of the type by 2 points which, on a book of this length, yielded a further 20,000 copies...

'Some heartburning was felt at the time that the American edition of each volume appeared a considerable length of time before the British edition, and an explanation of the cause of this would not be out of place. In the first instance, the British edition was more than three times as large as the American publisher's edition and therefore in any case took three times as long to print. Furthermore, the maps in the American edition were printed in black only, while those in the British edition were mostly in three colours.'[2]

The reduction of the type-size led to friction between author and publisher. Various friends wrote to Churchill with the acid remark that they would be delighted to read his book when they could find a magnifying glass, and Churchill passed on equally acerbic comments of his own. The Cassell directors rightly considered themselves justified, as a large number of people would have been disappointed had they not taken this step; but as paper rationing had just ended, they were able entirely to reset the first volume in a larger size for the second edition, and set all the succeeding volumes uniformly.

The actions of the Houghton Mifflin Company in refusing further corrections gave rise to the anomalous situation in which, although their edition is indisputably the first, it does not contain the approved text, even though Churchill does not seem actively to have disapproved. For the correct text, one must refer to the Cassell edition, or even the 'Chartwell' edition, though there is no certainty that Churchill personally corrected the proofs of the latter, beyond making a few revisions of fact.

So much for the general editorial situation. The detailed printing history of the British edition is, in its own way, equally complex. It is most convenient to take each volume separately and successively, starting at the point when printing started.

The first edition of Volume 1 consisted of 221,000 copies, of which 60,000 were printed by Ebenezer Baylis, and 161,000 by Wyman. The second edition of 100,000 copies, entirely reset as noted above, was split between Wyman and Chapel River Press of Andover, the former printing all sections except N and O.[3] This division of work also applied to the three following impressions (wrongly called 'editions' by Cassell), consisting of 50,000 (February, 1950), 5000 (March, 1955) and 10,000 copies (November, 1955) respectively.

The first impression of Volume II consisted of 276,000 copies. Wyman printed sections 2, 4, 12, 14 and 16 to 21 (numbers 2 and 4 being in three colours), Chapel River Press printed sections 3, 6 (three colours) and 9 (two colours); while Baylis dealt with sections 1, 5, 7, 8, 10, 11, 13, 15 and 22 (of which 5 and 12 were in colour), together with the three folding maps. This arrangement remained for the printing of the second impression of 25,000 copies in September, 1950. For the third impression of 25,000 in September, 1951, Chapel River was dropped, its sections going to Wyman (3 and 6) and Hazell, Watson and Viney (9). For the fourth impression of 5000 printed in October and November, 1954, section 9 was transferred to Wyman; and this position was retained for the fifth printing of 10,000 in December, 1955.

One impression only of 300,000 copies was printed in June, 1950, of the first edition of Volume III, the work being handled by Baylis, Chapel River, Greycaines, Wyman and Hazell.

One impression only of the first edition of Volume IV was printed in April and May, 1951, consisting of 275,000 copies. The work was split between the five firms who had handled the previous volume. Wyman printed sections A, D, G, J, K, M, R, S and Y (S and Y in two colours); Chapel River produced sections B, C, L and more of D (all in two colours); Greycaines printed sections 2D and 2E together with five folding maps; Hazell printed 128 pages in black and 64 pages in red and black; and Baylis printed 192 pages in black and 64 in red and black.[4]

The first and only impression of Volume V consisted of 275,000 copies, printed by the same five firms in June and July, 1952. Baylis printed sections A, C, D, E, F, H and four folding maps; Wyman printed sections J to Q; Hazell, sections T to W, and B in colour; Greycaines, sections G, X and Y; and Chapel River produced S in colour.

The first impression of Volume VI consisted of 200,000 copies, again produced by the same firms between February and April, 1954. Greycaines handled the eleven folding maps; Wyman printed sections K, L, N, O, S, T, U and V; Chapel River, sections F and H; Hazell, sections M, P and R; and

Baylis printed sections A to E, G, I, W, X and Y. The second impression, printed in the same way, consisted of a further 20,000 copies which were produced during October, 1954.

The dust-wrappers for all volumes were printed by West Brothers of Streatham, and the end-papers by Fletcher of Norwich. The binding was divided between Leighton Straker, G. and J. Kitcat, and Webb.

For the Cassell production staff it must have been a juggling act of unnerving complexity. It is surely a high compliment to them that the whole convoluted process went relatively smoothly.

THE BRITISH GAZETTE

No account of Churchill as a journalist would be complete without some mention of his editorial activities during the General Strike of 1926.

During the evening of 2 May, the day before the strike was due to start, several newspapers including the *Daily Mail* and *Daily Express* were either suppressed or censored by the machine-minders. Aware of the dangers of a muzzled Press, Stanley Baldwin, then Prime Minister, summoned Churchill to organize an emergency newspaper. As would be expected, he rose to the challenge with drive and imagination, laying down his guidelines in advance.

'...the essential thing is that we should produce a really powerful readable broadsheet not merely to contain news but in order to relieve the minds of the people....I do not contemplate violent partisanship, but fair, strong encouragement to the great mass of loyal people.'[1]

Questioned in detail about the visualised contents, he said: 'Obviously mainly of news, speeches, etc, also recruiting going on, anything occurring in the country organisations. But it should have a leading article, not violently partisan, but agreeable to the great majority of the people of our side: Constitutional, the hope for peace, Parliament maintains authority in the country, injury to trade and reputation of the country.'[2]

Leaving aside those indirectly reported sentiments, it is surely clear that what Churchill considered 'not violently partisan' would certainly be viewed as 'highly partisan' to those who were not 'people of our side'. Protestations notwithstanding, Churchill had no intention of editing an objective newspaper; as always, print was a powerful and valuable weapon.

By arrangement with the proprietors of the *Morning Post*, Churchill took over the building and set to work to produce the first edition of *The British Gazette*. The unions promptly pulled out their men but Churchill, rarely at a loss during a crisis, equally promptly called Lord Beaverbrook. Within an hour the night superintendent of the *Daily Express* was working the linotype machine single-handedly to produce the first issue on time. It consisted of only one leaf, printed on both sides, but it sold 232,000 copies.

From that moment the circulation had the sort of meteoric rise that conventional editors can only fantasize about; though, of course, there was no competition. During its mayfly existence its daily sales figures were: 232,000; 507,000; 655,000; 836,000; 1,117,600; 1,801,400; 2,209,000.

There was also a sister-paper, *The Sunday Gazette*. Smaller in format and consisting of one leaf printed on one side only, it was produced by a volunteer team from the offices of the *Islington Daily Gazette*. Only 7500 copies were produced, but these were sold out by 9am, and raised a grand revenue of £30.

After the strike, various miniature reprints of the *Gazette* were published as souvenirs and nowadays command astonishingly high prices, as do even tattered sets of the original newspaper. *The Sunday Gazette* was not included in the souvenir reprints.

During his editorship of *The British Gazette* Churchill wrote at least one article in every issue, though none was signed; a few were ascribed to 'Government sources' or described as 'official communiqués'. Even at that time, few people seem to have been taken in; on 10 May the *British Worker* accused Churchill of writing an article 'signed' by Balfour. Only by reference to the Churchill Archives can the editor's contributions be identified; there are, however, some highly characteristic, and therefore identifiable, passages, none more so than the valedictory statement in the issue of 13 May.

'*The British Gazette* may have had a short life; but it has fulfilled the purpose of living. It becomes a memory; but it remains a monument.'

In spite of pious preliminary statements, Churchill ran *The British Gazette* not merely as a medium for Government announcements and propaganda, but also as an avowedly strike-breaking weapon, to such an extent that in the subsequent Parliamentary debate, he was bitterly attacked by Labour MPs. His retort is one of his best-known; 'I utterly decline to be impartial as between the Fire Brigade and the fire.'

As an afternote, it is heartwarming to observe that, thanks to Churchill's impish sense of humour and timing, the debate that could so easily have ended in bitterness and division ended with the House being united in laughter.

'Speaking in the most dramatic tones in which defiance and solemnity were mingled and shaking his finger in a threatening manner at the Members of the Opposition, Mr Churchill, in a House that was tense with anticipation, delivered this solemn pronouncement:

' "One last word. The Honourable Member for the Forest of Dean has indicated that a time may come when another trial of strength will occur and when something like this will be tried again upon the country or the community. I have no wish to make threats or to use language which would disturb the House or cause bad blood. But this I must say: make your minds perfectly clear that if ever you loose upon us again a general strike, we will loose upon you — another *British Gazette*.'[3]

THE CONTRIBUTIONS OF
A. MARSHALL DISTON AND
EDWARD MARSH

Towards the end of 1933 Churchill embarked upon a process of literary cannibalization, turning old articles into new. Initially these were for the use of Amalgamated Press, and largely for their weekly publication *Answers*. In the course of this he began to develop a collaboration with the then Acting Editor of that magazine, Adam Marshall Diston.[1] At that early stage it seems that only relatively minor textual adjustments were made. Nevertheless, Churchill soon found himself threatened with the possibility of several actions for breach of contract. In a memorandum, his formidably efficient secretary Violet Pearman laid down the law.

'I was very much alarmed after my talk with Mr Diston of the Amalgamated Press on Friday to learn that they had taken no care at all to see if any rights were infringed on the reprinted and altered articles....

According to the files I have looked through:-

Daily Mail has bought British serial rights.

Strand has bought British Empire and American serial rights.

Nash's (probably the same, but nothing to show on the files which date back to 1926).

Hearst has bought the World serial rights.

Collier's have bought first American and Canadian serial rights.

'You will thus see that *Collier's* is the only safe one to reprint after alteration....

'The Amalgamated Press have... to date hashed 2 *Daily Mail* articles, two *Collier's*, three *Nash's*, 1 *Sunday Chronicle*....

'Some of the material used previously is beyond recall, already being incorporated in the magazines which are printed. This matter must be cleared up.'[2]

It remains unclear whether Churchill took any action to rectify this situation; it seems that he was unperturbed. Certainly he continued the process. Indeed, it very quickly becomes apparent that he and Diston between them had significantly widened its scope. On 25 November, 1934, Diston wrote to Violet Pearman:

'I am enclosing Chapters II and III of the Autobiography....Chapter III is all paraphrase except one folio....

'In all, there are roughly 5300 words of paraphrase in this batch — 1568 in Chapter II and 3785 in Chapter III, which now totals 3972 words....

'Then, in the case of Chapter III, I have inserted a new introductory paragraph, which, while containing the same idea as the original introduction, and at least one of its phrases, gives the impression of new matter more definitely than a stricter paraphrase would have done.'[3]

Clearly Diston had started adding his own words with the evident intention of enhancing the articles' spurious newness. Equally clearly, this was being done with Churchill's knowledge and approval, though whether he had initially briefed Diston to this effect, or whether he was merely content to accept a *fait accompli*, remains unknown.

Diston's letter to Violet Pearman of 20 August, 1935, adds another dimension:

'On the short biographies I think that, if Mr Churchill agrees, I might tackle first Clemenceau, French and Balfour.... By the way, I seem to have omitted to make a note of the length required. Was it 3000 words?'

Apart from these three, Diston also dealt with a profile of Lord Curzon. His letter about these reveals the extent to which he was actually writing original material for Churchill to pass off as his own.

'French: Here, again because it expresses the keynote of the article so admirably, the original introductory paragraph becomes paragraph two of the draft article. The rest of the first three pages is practically all new matter. Later in the article, in order to bring it to the required length, I have inserted an account of Lord Kitchener's visit to Paris in uniform and a few brief sentences on the last years of Lord Ypres' life....

'Curzon: As introduction I have extended the story of the disappointment over the Premiership, incorporating as much as possible of the shorter account in the original. Later, to bring the article to the required length, I have added rather more detail to the account of his Foreign Secretaryship and the fall of the Coalition....

'I hope that you will find the new matter satisfactory – I think I have managed to keep it in the spirit of the original in each case – and that the drafts will meet with your approval'.[4]

From this we can see not only that Diston was adding original material but was even doing so on his own decision, informing Churchill only after the articles had been completed. Consider the extent of the interpolation: in the article on French, only one paragraph in the first three typescript pages is actually written by Churchill. And there are further – and probably significant, if they were made to meet length requirements – additions towards the end. In the profile of Curzon, his additions are, by his own admission, *passim*.

Churchill had already written articles on these men in the late Twenties and early Thirties; they eventually appeared in *Great Contemporaries*. While it might *perhaps* be considered acceptable (though I do not believe so) for Churchill to behave in this fashion towards the transient Press world, it is hardly acceptable when it comes to a permanent and considered publication in book form.

It could possibly be argued, even at this stage, that these were relatively minor revisions of little or no significance, and that, anyway, if Churchill accepted them they were henceforth *ur*-Churchill. Unfortunately for this contention, Violet Pearman's letter to Diston of 26 October, 1935, blatantly puts the matter into a different league entirely.

'I am asked by Mr Churchill to send you herewith the article on Lloyd George. Mr Churchill says that this is the one he likes the least, as the fitting in of the reviews does not hang at all well with your own material. *Would you therefore please put in much more of your own composition, as it is so good.'* [my italics]

How far, then, was Churchill prepared to go in foisting another man's writing on the public as his own? 'Please put in much more...' This is a long way indeed from the mere cannibalization with which the relationship started. Now we are into a question of ethics, not only in this matter but also in the parallel area of the erosion of subsidiary rights purchased earlier in good faith by publications on both sides of the Atlantic.

This, as it stands, would have been dishonest enough. It seems evident, however, that in the later stages of the collaboration, Churchill was happy to connive even further. As far, in fact, as having Diston write complete original articles for him. In his letter of 3 April, 1938, Diston wrote:

'I am enclosing draft of the German colonies article, 'Germany Wants a Place in the Sun.'... I propose to do next the article on the shipbuilding race and Japan.

' "Germany Wants a Place in the Sun" is again on the long side. But there are some references to Germany's colonial record which Mr Churchill may think go a bit too far, though they are based on official sources.'[5]

In his reply (dated the same day) Churchill's briefing clearly relates to *writing* rather than editing.

'This requires completely recasting and the introduction of perhaps a thousand words of new matter. It should feature the more prominent psychological contrasts between Hitler and Mussolini. It should also be brought up to date by reference to the last performances of both....This is only a guide. It should be easy to do this.'

In all his major works, with the exception of *Lord Randolph Churchill*, Churchill employed teams of research assistants. Possibly to him his use of Diston was merely more of the same. But it was certainly not the same either in action or intention. From the evidence laid out, I would regard it as proven that the initial cannibalization of his own texts eventually led Churchill into the deliberate use of a ghost-writer to produce complete articles for him. And should any doubts still linger in any minds, it is possible to find, tucked discreetly into the middle of a lengthy footnote, a categorical statement by Martin Gilbert: '...several of Churchill's published articles...were written in their entirety by Diston.'[6]

This is not merely a question of conning the public; it is also one of defrauding the editors of the journals concerned, who paid Churchillian fees for the work of an unknown hack.

As to extent, this remains uncertain. I would, however, propose that the following articles are identifiable as corrupt, in the sense that they are wholly or partly written by Diston:

'How We Made the Irish Treaty' *Pictorial Weekly*, 20 January, 1934.

'Will the League Survive?' *Pictorial Weekly*, 27 January, 1934.

'If I Could Live my Life Again' *Pictorial Weekly*, 3 February, 1934.

' "Be Prepared" – and the Man who Thought of it' *Daily Mail*, 6 March, 1934.

'Have You a Hobby?' *Answers*, 21 April, 1934.

'Let's Boost Britain' *Answers*, 28 April, 1934.
'When I "Dried Up" ' *Pictorial Weekly*, 26 May, 1934.
'Dramatic Days in "the House" ' *Pictorial Weekly*, 2 June, 1934.
'I *Always* Took Chances' *Answers*, 30 June, 1934.
'My Life' *News of the World*, 13 January to 31 March, 1935.
'Great Men of our Time' *News of the World*, 12 January to 5 April, 1936.
'The Great Reigns' London *Evening Standard*, 26 April to 3 May, 1937.
    (probably derived from the preliminary draft of *A History
        of the English-Speaking Peoples*)
'Kitchener' *Sunday Chronicle*, 31 October 1937.
'My Life and Times' *Sunday Chronicle*, 5 December, 1937 to 13 February, 1938.
'Dictators on Dynamite' *Collier's*, 3 September, 1938.
'The Colony Racket' *Collier's*, 19 November, 1938.

Of these I am reasonably confident, but I am equally confident that an exhaustive comparison of texts published during the Twenties and Thirties would produce considerably more.

In view of all this, I have felt it also necessary to examine in more detail another journalistic project upon which I merely touched in the course of Chapter VI.

At the beginning of August 1932, Churchill accepted a commission from Lord Riddell, Chairman of the *News of the World*, to write six (later increased to twelve) 5000-word features retelling some of the world's great stories. The fee was £2000 for British serial rights plus a bonus for prompt delivery.

On the day that the agreement was made, Churchill wrote to Edward Marsh: 'It seems to me that you might help me in this task. If I had read about 2500 words of your ideas on each of the selected books it would be a foundation on which I could tell the story.'[7]

In his biography of Marsh, Christopher Hassall wrote that 'Marsh was invited to make a *précis* of each plot.... This was to prove a more elaborate undertaking than at first appeared.' It certainly was, and the reason for the unexpected complexity was that it quickly became apparent that Churchill did *not* want mere *préces*; he wanted something far more convenient to his purpose.

'I want to point out how hopeless it is to try and reduce these great works proportionately chapter by chapter to a smaller compass. Hundreds of pages have to be obliterated as if they had never been written. Only the salient counts and must be told fully enough to hold their full dramatic content.'[8]

In other words, what he wanted was a complete editorial restructuring. At the time he was deeply engrossed in *Marlborough* and had other journalistic commitments, so it could be argued that he was merely using Marsh as he used Ashley and others — as a devil. If this were so, the situation would be unexceptionable. It is Marsh's own words, however, particularly viewed in the light of the Diston collaboration, that throw some doubt on this interpretation.

The first hint that Marsh was, in fact, going well beyond his initial brief comes in his letter to Churchill of 12 November, 1932. 'I'm now hard at work at Ben-Hur, & nearly half through it. Golly, what a book! The seafight is really fun, so I'm making that a "high-light", & there will be another in the chariot race.'

It seems apparent from this, I believe, that Marsh was not producing either ideas or *préces*, but was actually using creative language and techniques (I'm making that a "high-light" ') rather than merely summarizing. Churchill's reply two days later implicitly confirms this suspicion: 'I think it is only necessary to select the main episodes, and not to tell the story evenly and conscientiously throughout.' The original request merely for ideas seems to have been jettisoned, and the use of the phrase 'tell the story' is extremely revealing. Churchill is wanting structure, interpretation and presentation delivered pre-packaged to his desk.

A few days later an even stronger confirmation emerges in Churchill's letter to Marsh of 26 November: 'I am much pleased with Ben-Hur though it amounted to over 7000 [words] when they are all counted up, and I still have to prune 1500.'

Prune? To prune is to cut; by no means to rewrite. Was Churchill then taking Marsh's texts and using them as his own? And why, suddenly, have the '2500 words of ideas' become 7000?

That Marsh was deliberately writing versions to the 5000-word length required by the *News of the World* is surely made crystal-clear in two further letters to Churchill. 'Here is Adam Bede, for once I have got it within 5000 words!' (21 January, 1933.) 'Here is Westward Ho!...The bill says it's exactly 5000 words for once.' (24 February, 1933.)

Further, it is surely significant that at no time does Marsh say, 'Here are the notes for...'; simply 'Here is ...'

And on 22 February Churchill sent Marsh a cheque 'for the four drafts you have so kindly done for me'. *Drafts*, not notes or *préces* or ideas: *drafts*. And a draft, according to the relevant definition in the *Oxford English Dictionary*, is 'a rough form whence a fair copy can be made'. The inference can only be that, for Churchill, Marsh's texts needed little if any work, if not absolutely final texts, then precious close to that condition.

One final and very tangential point. Churchill paid Marsh £25 for each text, giving him £300 for a few weeks' part-time work. Yet at approximately the same time he was paying Maurice Ashley exactly the same sum on an *annual half-time basis* for work that was considerably more demanding. If Ashley was not being considerably underpaid, than Marsh was being considerably overpaid – unless, of course, he was producing something a good deal more substantial that mere 'ideas'.

All this, is I admit, largely inferential; and, were it not for the fact that Churchill was quite prepared to pass off others' work as his own, I doubt if I would have suspected that here might be another example. But in that light, and given that Marsh had already written a successful and acknowledged Churchill pastiche in the introduction to *Thoughts and Adventures*, it is difficult not to be – *at the very least* – extremely suspicious.

WORKS CONSULTED

(a) Works by Sir Winston Churchill

The Story of the Malakand Field Force
(1898)
The River War (1899)
Savrola (1900)
London to Ladysmith via Pretoria (1900)
Ian Hamilton's March (1900)
Mr Brodrick's Army (1903)
Lord Randolph Churchill (1906)
For Free Trade (1906)
My African Journey (1908)
Liberalism and the Social Problem
(1909)
The People's Rights (1910)
The World Crisis (1923-31)
My Early Life (1930)
India (1931)
Thoughts and Adventures (1932)
Marlborough: His Life and Times
(1933-38)
Great Contemporaries (1937)
Arms and the Covenant (1938)
Step by Step (1939)
Into Battle (1941)
The Unrelenting Struggle (1942)

The End of the Beginning (1943)
Onwards to Victory (1944)
The Dawn of Liberation (1945)
Victory (1946)
Secret Session Speeches (1946)
The Second World War (1948-54)
The Second World War (one-volume
abridged edition with Epilogue,
1959)
The Sinews of Peace (1948)
Painting as a Pastime (1948)
Europe Unite (1950)
In the Balance (1951)
Stemming the Tide (1953)
A History of the English-Speaking
Peoples (1956-58)
The Unwritten Alliance (1961)

Young Winston's Wars (ed. Frederick
Woods, 1974)
The Complete Speeches (ed. Robert
Rhodes James, 1974)
Collected Essays (ed. Michael Woolf,
1976)

(b) Other Works

ASHLEY, MAURICE: *Marlborough* (Duckworth 1939)
    Churchill as Historian (Secker and Warburg 1968)
BERLIN, ISAIAH: *Mr Churchill in Bern* (Murray 1964)
BONHAM-CARTER, VIOLET: *Winston Churchill as I Knew Him* (Eyre and
    Spottiswoode with Collins 1965)
BULLARD, F. LAURISTON: *Famous War Correspondents* (Little Brown 1914)
CAMERON, NORMAN and STEVENS, R.H. (ed): *Hitler's Table Talk*
    (Weidenfeld and Nicolson 1953)
CHURCHILL, RANDOLPH: *(Winston S. Churchill,* Vols. I-II (Heinemann 1966-67)
CHURCHILL, SARAH: *A Thread in the Tapestry* (Deutsch 1967)
COCKETT, R.: *Twilight of Truth* (Weidenfeld and Nicolson 1989)
CRUTTWELL, C.R.M.F.: *A History of the Great War 1914-1918 (Clarendon Press 1934)*

d'ARCOS, JOAQUIN PACO: *Churchill – the Statesman and Writer* (Caravel Press 1957)

DEAKIN, FREDERICK W.: *Churchill the Historian* (University of Basle 1969)

EADE, CHARLES (ed): *Churchill by his Contemporaries* (Hutchinson 1953)

'EPHESIAN': *Winston Churchill* (Mills and Boon 1927)

FOSTER, R.F.: *Lord Randolph Churchill: a Political Life* (Clarendon Press 1981)

GILBERT, MARTIN: *Winston S. Churchill*, Vols. III-VIII (Heinemann 1971-)

HARRIS, FRANK: *My Life and Loves* (W.H. Allen 1964)

HASSALL, CHRISTOPHER: *Edward Marsh* (Longman 1959)
                             Ambrosia and Small Beer (Longman 1964)

HAY, MALCOLM V.: *Winston Churchill and James II: a Criticism of Marlborough* (Harding and More 1934)

JAMES, ROBERT RHODES: *Lord Randolph Churchill* (Weidenfeld and Nicolson 1959)
                             Churchill: a Study in Failure (Weidenfeld and Nicolson 1970)

LUDOVICI, L.F.: *Nobel Prize Winners* (Arco 1957)

MACAULAY, T.B.: *History of England* (London 1849-55)

MARSH, EDWARD: *A Number of People* (Heinemann with Hamish Hamilton 1939)

MARTIN, RALPH G.: *Lady Randolph Churchill* (Cassell 1969)

MOIR, PHYLLIS: *I was Winston Churchill's Private Secretary* (Funk 1941)

MORAN, LORD: *Winston Churchill: the Struggle for Survival* (Constable 1966)

NEL, ELIZABETH: *Mr Churchill's Secretary* (Hodder and Stoughton 1958)

NOWELL-SMITH, SIMON: *The House of Cassell* (Cassell 1958)

PELLING, HENRY: *Winston Churchill* (Macmillan 1974)

POUND, REGINALD: *The Strand Magazine* (Heinemann 1966)

ROSEBERY, LORD: *Lord Randolph Churchill* (A.L. Humphreys 1906)

ROWSE, A.L.: *The Early Churchills* (Macmillan 1956)
                      The English Spirit (Macmillan 1945)

SCOTT, A. McCALLUM: *Winston Spencer Churchill* (Methuen 1905)

STEWART, H.L.: *Winston Churchill as Writer and Speaker (Sidgwick and Jackson 1954)*

THOMSON, G.M.: *The First Churchill* (Secker and Warburg 1979)

VARIOUS: *Churchill: Four Faces and the Man* (Allen Lane 1969)
            The World Crisis by Winston Churchill: a Criticism (Hutchinson 1924)

WEIDHORN, MANFRED: *Sword and Pen* (University of New Mexico Press 1974)

WOODS, FREDERICK: *A Bibliography of the Works of Sir Winston Churchill*, 4th ed. (St Paul's Bibliographies)
            Young Winston's Wars (Leo Cooper 1974)

NOTES

OB: *Winston S. Churchill* by Randolph S. Churchill (Vols. I-II) and Martin Gilbert (Vols. III-VIII), the Official Biography.

Introduction

1. Quoted in Earl of Oxford and Asquith: *Memories and Reflections.*
2. 'Churchill the Journalist,' in *Churchill by his Contemporaries.*
3. *Churchill: Four Faces and the Man,* pp. 139-40.
4. 'Life,' Churchill said to Moran towards the end of his days, 'life has been too full of things to read much.'

Chapter I

1. Letter dated 5 August, 1893. Lord Randolph was already in the grip of the tertiary syphilis which finally killed him. Six generations of Spencer-Churchills had been at Eton, and he was under the delusion that his son had also been there. In fact, Churchill had been kept away from Eton because it was feared that its low-lying position would be injurious to his health.
2. Letter dated 12 July, 1888.
3. Letter dated 9 August, 1893. There seems almost to have been a family tradition at work here. While at Eton, Lord Randolph himself was on the receiving end of an equally harsh letter from the Duke of Marlborough. 'It really is too annoying that after all our kindness to you, to be subjected to this kind of anxiety about you... I have too frequently had to complain of impertinence & overbearing disposition. There is nothing in the world which is so low and contemptible and makes a boy and subsequently a man so *justly* detestable.'

   And, in his turn, Churchill rounded on *his* son. 'I grieve more than is worth setting down to see you with so many gifts & so much good treatment from the world leading the life of a selfish exploiter, borrowing & spending every shilling you can lay yr hands on, & ever-increasing the lavish folly of your way. But words are useless.' (Letter of 3 November, 1931.)
4. Letter dated 4 October, 1887.
5. Letter dated 14 December, 1887.
6. Letter dated 14 February, 1888.
7. Essay dated 26 May, 1888.
8. *Ibid.*
9. Letter dated 19 September, 1891.
10. Early in the Second World War, Churchill's propaganda machine provided him with the deflating statement that Hitler was actually called Schickelgruber. One can equate the smear with the 'traditional' song that begins 'Hitler has only got one ball'. In wartime any weapon counts, no matter how trivial. See also note 17 to Chapter VI.
11. Letter to *The Harrovian,* 17 March, 1892.
12. Letter to *The Harrovian,* 17 November, 1892.
13. Letter to *The Harrovian,* 15 June, 1893.

Chapter II

1. Mrs Ormiston Chant (1848-1923) was a hospital matron and assistant manager of a private lunatic asylum, and was involved in women's suffrage, temperance, purity and Liberal politics. She was the author of a book of short sermons, a novel, many poems and children's songs. She was also, it seems, proficient at billiards.

   The Empire Theatre was notorious at that time for the many prostitutes and other undesirables who frequented it.
2. Letter dated 25 October, 1894.
3. Letter dated 31 August, 1895.
4. *Daily Graphic,* 13 December, 1895.
5. *Daily Graphic,* 17 December, 1895.
6. *Daily Graphic,* 13 December, 1895.
7. *Daily Graphic,* 27 December, 1895.
8. *My Early Life,* chapter 4.
9. *Daily Graphic,* 13 January, 1896.
10. *Ibid.*
11. Churchill did not actually receive his medal until 1914, when it was presented to him by King Alfonso XIII. He was not permitted to wear it, and it is not included in the family's framed set of his decorations.
12. Churchill also sent rough sketches which were redrawn for publication by one of the *Graphic's* staff artists, T.C. Crowther.
13. The Jameson Raid had recently taken place.
14. Published 15 February, entitled 'The Revolt in Cuba.' Two more followed in the same magazine on 7 March and 29 August.
15. Letter dated 21 June, 1896.
16. Letter dated 7 January, 1897.
17. Letter to Lady Randolph dated 14 April, 1897.
18. Letter to Lady Randolph dated 14 January, 1897.
19. Letter dated 14 February, 1897.
20. Moreton Frewen (1853-1924). Related to the Churchills through his marriage to Clara Jerome. Author of several works on bimetallism. MP for N.E. Cork 1910-11.
21. Letter dated 21 April, 1897.
22. Letter dated 21 April, 1897.
23. Letter dated 28 April, 1897.
24. The quotation offers an interesting contrast to his sentiments about writing for money, expressed to his grandmother.
25. Letter dated 25 October, 1897.
26. *Daily Telegraph,* 6 October, 1897.
27. *Daily Telegraph,* 19 November, 1897.
28. *Daily Telegraph,* 6 November, 1897.
29. *Daily Telegraph,* 13 November, 1897.
30. Letter to Lady Randolph dated 21 October, 1897.
31. Letter dated 17 November, 1897.
32. Letter dated 9 December, 1897.
33. Letter dated 22 December, 1897. The last sentence is a reference to Lady Randolph's financial problems.
34. Letter dated 31 December, 1897.
35. Letter dated 10 January, 1898.
36. Letter dated 27 January, 1898.
37. Letter dated 27 January, 1898.

Chapter III

1. *My Early Life,* chapter 13.
2. Cable of ? July, 1898.
3. Letter dated 11 January, 1899.
4. Letter dated 6 October, 1898.
5. *Morning Post,* 6 October, 1898.
6. *Ibid.*
7. *The River War,* Vol. II, p. 195.
8. Ibid, pp. 193-4. One cannot help wondering whether the young Haig might not have taken that last sentence to heart, and rediscovered it during the Battle of the Somme.
9. *Ibid,* pp. 377-78.
10. Letter dated ?7 July, 1899. Over thirty years later, Churchill had the grace and the sense of humour to reprint the comments in *My Early Life* with minor textual variants.

11. Indicative of Churchill's altered stance is his later statement that 'Lord Kitchener was greater as a man than as a general.' (*Illustrated Sunday Herald*, 25 April, 1920.) In view of later revelations of Kitchener's character, notably his blatant kleptomania, this is doubly ironic.

12. OB, Vol. I, pp. 449-50.

13. *Morning Post,* 25 July, 1900.

14. *Ibid,* 19 March, 1900.

15. Extract from the *Tugela ?Twaddle.* Quoted in OB, Vol. I, Comp. Vol. I, p. 1153. It is difficult to be sure whether the format arises from the limitations of a narrow column width or from a desire to write blank verse. Whichever it is, I have retained the setting used in OB.

16. *Morning Post,* 10 April, 1900.

17. *Ibid,* 11 April, 1900.

18. Undated letter, *c* 11 July, 1900.

19. In a letter to his mother dated 1 January, 1901, after his first American lecture tour, Churchill was able to claim 'I am very proud of the fact that there is not one person in a million who at my age could have earned £10,000 without any capital in less than two years.'

20. *Morning Post,* 12 July, 1900.

21. *Ibid,* 6 February, 1900.

22. 'Churchill the War Correspondent' in *Churchill by his Contemporaries.*

23. *Young Winston's Wars,* edited by Frederick Woods, 1974.

24. Broadcast review, BBC Radio 4, 1974.

Chapter IV

1. Letter dated 29 August, 1897.

2. Letter dated 19 September, 1897.

3. Letter dated 25 February, 1898.

4. Letter dated 29 November, 1898, and one with distinct overtones of Lady Bracknell!

5. A passage remarkably reminiscent of Lord Randolph's vitriolic letter to his son dated 9 August, 1893.

6. Letter dated 1 January, 1899.

Chapter V

1. For instance, there is a considerable difference in both attitude and function between Churchill's irreverent 'Some chicken, some neck' and the patronising arrogance of Macmillan's 'You've never had it so good'.

2. William Bourke Cockran (1854-1923). Irish-born American lawyer, politician and fiery orator. Democratic Member of Congress for New York 1891-5, 1904-9, 1920-23.

3. For a discussion of Churchill's writing methods, see Appendix I.

4. Churchill apparently viewed these changes with a sometimes sardonic eye. In a letter to his wife dated 13 April, 1935, he wrote, 'At sixty I am altering my method of speaking, largely under Randolph's tuition, and now talk to the House of Commons with garrulous unpremeditated flow. They seem delight- ed. But what a mystery the art of public speaking is! It all consists in my (mature) judgment of assembling three or four absolutely sound arguments and putting these in the most conversational manner possible. There is apparently nothing in the literary effect I have sought for forty years!'

William Carlos Williams developed a typographical layout in his poems which resembled that of Churchill's notes; a facsimile can be found on pp. 8-16 of *Secret Session Speeches.*

5. William St John Fremantle Brodrick (1856-1942). Secretary of State for War 1900-03. Created 1st Earl of Midleton 1920.

6. Speech at Oldham, 19 January, 1903.

7. Speech at Wallsend, 13 February, 1903.

8. Arthur L. Humphreys was the then manager of Hatchard's bookshop in Piccadilly.

9. Published by the Library of Imperial History.

10. Speech at Birmingham, 10 January, 1910.

11. Speech at Dundee, 15 January, 1910.

12. Recent disclosures regarding Anglo-German relations during the Thirties have demonstrated just how deeply entrenched the pro-Hitler governmental faction was. Throughout Chamberlain's period as Prime Minister, his Press Secretary George Steward was in regular direct contact with the German Embassy in London, giving them inside information on governmental attitudes and discussions. Whether Chamberlain knew of this surely treasonable activity or not, the fact that it continued for so long is a clear indication of the depth of pro-German feeling that existed in the British government at that time.

For Churchill to adopt the stance he did and maintain it alone for so long was not therefore merely a question of being regarded as an unnecessary alarmist; it was, in fact, to be regarded in some quarters as a deliberate anti-government mischief-maker if nothing worse.

It is small wonder that Steward was dismissed by Churchill immediately he succeeded Chamberlain.

See Richard Cockett: *Twilight of Truth* (Weidenfeld 1989.)

13. Speech at the Royal Albert Hall, 18 March, 1931.

14. *Step by Step* is considered under Journalism.

15. Speech in the House of Commons, 25 May, 1938.

16. Speech in the House of Commons, 5 October, 1938.

17. *Into Battle* took its title from Julian Grenfell's First World War poem, though the reference was not made clear until the seventh 'edition' – I use the publisher's incorrect designation – when a quotation was inserted on the title-page.

18. Except for a small pamphlet entitled *Prison and Prisoners* (1910) when Churchill was Home Secretary.

19. Between 1940 and 1944 the Political Warfare Executive printed many hundreds of leaflets, booklets and magazines which were dropped over Europe. Many of these reprinted or quoted from Churchill's speeches and, occasionally, included a specially written item. An almost complete collection is held by the Imperial War Museum, and background information can be found in Sir Robert H. Bruce Lockhart's *Comes the Reckoning* (Putnam 1947).

For further details see Woods: *A Bibliography of the Works of Sir Winston Churchill,* Appendix II.

20. Speech broadcast by the BBC, 29 November, 1942.

21. Speech in London on VE Day, 8 May, 1945.

22. Speech broadcast by the BBC, 13 May, 1945.

23. To describe an edition of 5000 as indicative of a 'decline' may seem to some to suggest ignorance of the practice and economics of publishing. The figure should be taken in conjunction with the fact that the first printing *only* of the first volume of *The Second World War* was 221,000.

24. As early as 15 February, 1930, the *Saturday Evening Post* published an article by Churchill entitled 'The United States of Europe'. It appeared in Britain simultaneously in *John Bull* entitled 'A Great Big Idea'.

25. Rosebery: *Lord Randolph Churchill,* pp. 82-3.

Chapter VI

1. Among the former were such articles as 'Some Impressions of the War in South Africa' (*Journal of the Royal United Services Institution,* July, 1901) and 'A Danger to the Empire' (*Daily Mail,* 16, 17 and 19 December, 1904.) In the latter category were a six-part series in *The London Magazine,* October 1916-March, 1917, entitled 'The War by Land and Sea,' and a succession of articles in the *Sunday Pictorial* between July, 1916 and July, 1917.

2. There was also a project, possibly fortunately abortive, to retell the Bible.

3. Reginald Pound: *The Strand Magazine* (Heinemann, 1966).

4. Lord Moran: *Winston Churchill: the Struggle for Survival* (Constable, 1966). 'Nineteen and six' equals 97½p.

5. 'My New York Misadventure,' *Daily Mail,* 4 and 5 January, 1932. Professor Lindemann (later Lord Cherwell) supplied the calculations.

6. Kenneth Young: *Churchill and Beaverbrook* (Eyre and Spottiswoode, 1966).

7. Phyllis Moir: *I was Winston Churchill's Private Secretary* (Funk, 1941).

8. Moran: *op cit.* The present-day value of £20,000 would be over £500,000.

9. R. Greenhough Smith, then Editor of *The Strand Magazine.*

10. OB Vol. II, Comp. Vol. 2, p. 741.

11. *My African Journey,* chapter 6.

12. Ibid, chapter 8.

13. For both this article and 'Fifty Years Hence', Churchill turned to Professor Lindemann for his information. In a letter dated 3 April, 1924, he wrote: 'I have undertaken to write on the future possibilities of war and how frightful it will be for the human race. On this subject I have a good many ideas, but I would very much like to have another talk with you following on the most interesting one we had when you last lunched here.' Churchill's letter to Lindemann dated 11 February, 1931 acknowledges the Professor's contribution to the later article.

Churchill's (or Lindemann's) ideas were actually largely pre-empted by H.G. Wells in his *Anticipations* (Chapman and Hall, 1902).

14. Churchill had, after all, made a point of telling the nation what it did not particularly want to hear.

15. 'Britain's Deficiencies in Aircraft Manufacture,' *Daily Telegraph,* 28 April, 1938. Reprinted in *Step by Step.*

16. 'The Crunch,' *Daily Telegraph,* 24 March, 1939. Reprinted in *Step by Step.*

17. Pound: *op cit.* The German Ambassador to Britain was at that time Joachim von Ribbentrop.

There is no doubt that Churchill's unceasing attacks angered Hitler intensely. During dinner with Rommel on 18 February, 1942, he erupted, 'Churchill is the very type of a corrupt journalist. There is not a worse prostitute in politics. He himself has written that it's unimaginable what can be done in war with the help of lies. He's an utterly amoral repulsive creature.'

Comment is superfluous.

18. In fact, these articles — together with another entitled 'What do you Know about Yourself' — were not published until 1942, when they appeared in the *Sunday Dispatch* headed by the statement that they had been written before the war but not previously published.

19. The proposed volume was prepared by the present writer and submitted to Churchill with suggestions for updating certain biographical essays. At a number of points Churchill wrote 'Certainly' or 'By all means' to these proposals. In the event, the texts were included in the *Collected Essays* (Library of Imperial History 1976.)

20. *P.T.O.,* 16 and 23 June, 1906.

21. 'Great Fighters in Lost Causes,' *Strand Magazine*, March, 1933.

22. *The Sunday Times*, 31 January, 1966. It was used as the basis of the closing scene in the film *Young Winston*.

Chapter VII

1. His practice of assembling teams of expert advisers began in 1920, when he started work on *The World Crisis*.

2. Letter dated 19 January. George Curzon, later 4th Earl Howe and not to be confused with George Nathaniel Curzon of Kedleston, was one of the Trustees of Lord Randolph's papers, together with the MP Ernest Beckett. The financial estimate was for once an understatement.

3. Letter dated 10 June, 1902. Sir Michael Hicks Beach (later Earl St Aldwyn, 1837-1916) was a fellow-parliamentarian and close friend of Lord Randolph.

4. Letter dated 15 August, 1902.

5. Undated (September, 1902) letter to Ernest Beckett.

6. Or *was* it 'stunning honesty'? Goschen was, of course, the man Lord Randolph 'forgot' in his calculations preceding his resignation, and the phrase 'I forgot Goschen' was in common circulation after the event. It is impossible not to wonder whether his response to the son might not have been a gentle ironic revenge.

7. Neither the appointment nor the eventual personal profits stopped Harris writing of Lord Randolph with the utmost salaciousness in *My Life and Loves* (1922-27). In spite of the fact that the episode described may well be very relevant to Lord Randolph's fatal infection (if, indeed, it is not purely a product of Harris's fevered imagination), the gutter-writing is such as totally to alienate any serious researcher.

8. Letters to William Heinemann and Sir Algernon Methuen dated 10 October, 1905.

9. Lord Rosebery, *Lord Randolph Churchill*, p. 5.

10. Leader of the Dervishes, whose tomb was desecrated by Kitchener at the culmination of the Sudan campaign in 1898.

11. Rosebery, *op cit*, p. 182. He goes on to say, 'His son has wisely not shrunk from setting down some of the abuse of which he was the object, and it all now seems trivial enough.' Churchill's references, however, are mostly concerned with Press cartoons, and such insults as he quotes are in a different league from Rosebery's. They are, indeed, 'trivial enough', but they represent yet another distortion on Churchill's part.

12. *Daily Telegraph*, 2 January, 1906. The last phrase may refer to his attempted blackmail of the Prince of Wales in 1876 which led to a lengthy ostracism by the Royal Family and those who followed their dictates.

13. 'The history of the Fourth Party has been written by Mr Harold Gorst... with a natural desire to point out that it was not entirely composed of Randolph.' Rosebery, *op cit*, p. 144.

14. Rosebery, *op cit*, pp. 144-5.

15. Piggott had forged the documents purporting to link Parnell with the Phoenix Park murders. He subsequently committed suicide in Lisbon, having fled the country.

16. The stanza comes from the poem *Hohenlinden* by Thomas Campbell (1777-1844), hardly one of our greatest English poets, though it was he, and not Byron, who coined the phrase beloved of authors everywhere: 'Now Barabbas was a publisher...' Campbell actually wrote 'Wave, Munich...'

17. Winston S. Churchill: *Lord Randolph Churchill*, Vol. II, pp. 465-6.

18. Rosebery, *op cit*, p. 99. This passage – and in particular the way in which he refers to 'the hallucination of disease' – suggests that Rosebery might have been party to the secret.

19. *My Early Life*, p. 32.

20. Winston S. Churchill, *op cit,* Vol. II, pp. 488-9.
21. Malcolm Muggeridge in *Churchill by his Contemporaries.*
22. Letter dated 14 November, 1928.
23. A consideration of Churchill's research and writing methods is to be found at Appendix I.
24. Speech at Harrap luncheon, 4 October, 1933.
25. Macaulay: *History of England,* Vol. III, chapter XX.
26. Churchill: *Marlborough,* Vol. I, p. 18. This reference, and all subsequent *Marlborough* references, applies to the two-volume edition published in 1947.
27. As note 24.
28. It seems, however, as if Churchill's rejection of Macaulay's views was selective. In his slim but pointed book *Winston Churchill and James II,* Malcolm V. Hays makes detailed criticisms of Churchill's treatment of James and, ironically, accuses him of blind adherence to Macaulay's biased picture of the King.
29. Ashley: *Marlborough,* p. 13.
30. Churchill: *op cit,* Vol. I, pp. 221-2.
31. *Ibid,* Vol. I, p. 252.
32. *Ibid,* Vol. I, p. 262.
33. *Ibid,* Vol. II, pp. 499-500. The Marquis d'Alègre was captured in July, 1705, when the Lines of Brabant were overrun by Marlborough's cavalry. Marlborough gave him two months' parole to settle his affairs, and at the same time sent Louis XIV respectful and friendly greetings. On his return Alègre brought news of the bribe.
34. *Ibid,* Vol. II, p. 500.
35. *Ibid,* Vol. II, p. 632.
36. Portland Papers, Historical Manuscripts Commission, iv, 27.
37. Churchill: *Marlborough,* Vol. II, p. 633.
38. *Ibid,* Vol. II, p. 626.
39. *Ibid,* Vol. II, p. 628.
40. *Ibid,* Vol. II, p. 629.
41. Ashley: *Churchill as Historian,* p. 18.
42. 'The Duke of Marlborough,' *Blackwood's Magazine,* June, 1859, reprinted in *The New 'Examen.'*
43. 'History,' in *Miscellaneous Writings,* Vol. I, p. 233. (1828 edition.)
44. Malcolm Muggeridge in *Churchill by his Contemporaries.*

Chapter VIII

1. Letter dated 4 February, 1922. Thornton Butterworth recouped its advance within a year. But, alas for Churchill's careful sums, the book was finally published at 30/-!

   Younger readers confused by, and seeking an explanation of, pre-decimal currency might like to know that 31/6 equals 1½ guineas, 21/- a guinea, and 10/6 a half-guinea.
2. The specific reference of the proposed title was to Britain, as is made clear in *The World Crisis,* Vol. I, p. 503.
3. *The World Crisis,* Vol. I, p. 6.
4. *Ibid,* Vol. I, p. 7.
5. *Ibid,* Vol. II, p. 9.
6. Those who appreciate the finer points of hypocrisy will doubtless relish the fact that, on 6 March, 1929, Balfour wrote to Churchill: 'Five volumes of immortal history is a wonderful addition to this great period of administrative activity.'

   Other views were equally subjective, notably an apparently high-powered attack entitled *The World Crisis by Winston Churchill: A Criticism* (Hutchinson 1924), written by two generals, a colonel, an admiral, and the historian Sir Charles Oman. The value of this book can perhaps be judged from its laudatory references to 'the measured pages of Sir W. Robertson's revealing book'. If any senior officer should have kept quiet after the First World War it was surely Robertson.
7. *The World Crisis,* Vol. I, pp. 10-11.

8. Ibid, Vol. II, p. 500. The passage irresistibly recalls Shaw's comment in *The Devil's Disciple:* 'The British soldier can stand up to anything except the British War Office.'

9. *Ibid,* Vol. II, p. 11.

10. *Ibid,* Vol. II, p. 489.

11. *Ibid,* Vol. II, pp. 505-6.

12. There seems to be some confusion regarding the structure of *The World Crisis.* Some catalogues list it as a four-volume work in five volumes, some as a six-volume work in five, and yet others as a straight six-volume work. This divergence of views stems from the fact that (a) Volume III was published in two parts; and (b) *The Eastern Front* was not visualized in the original conception but published later.

   Bibliographically speaking, it is a five-volume work in six.

13. *The World Crisis,* Vol. III, p. 11.

14. *Ibid,* Vol. III, p. 11.

15. *Churchill: Four Faces and the Man,* p. 146.

16. *The World Crisis,* Vol. III, pp. 182-3. Clearly Churchill liked this description, since he took it word for word from his article 'Some Reflections on the Strategy of the Allies,' published in the American magazine *Century* as early as May, 1917.

17. *Ibid,* Vol. IV, pp. 454-5.

18. *Ibid,* Vol. IV, p. 451.

19. *Ibid,* Vol. IV, p. 459.

20. *Churchill as Historian,* p. 122.

21. Moran: *Winston Churchill: the Struggle for Survival,* p. 786.

22. Sir John Colville (1915-1987) was Cabinet Secretary during the war.

23. Revealingly, this was the only volume in which the Americans could not read about themselves!

24. That there was a recognised correlation between Churchill's decisions and the historical instincts that imbued them is indicated in his telegram from Paris to the War Cabinet dated 16 May, 1940. Referring to the French request for six extra fighter squadrons, he wrote, 'It would not be good historically if their requests were denied and their ruin resulted'. Later he used the portentous phrase 'the mortal quality of this hour'.

   This telegram caused some resentment in his Private Office. One member referred to 'blasted rhetoric', while another commented, 'He's still thinking of his books'.

   'Mortal quality', or not, Churchill reversed his decision three days later and withdrew all fighters from France.

25. *Churchill as Historian,* p. 37.

26. *The Second World War,* Vol. II, p. 555.

27. And yet by this time he had compromised the code: Coventry and Dresden provide the evidence.

28. Edward Marsh: *A Number of People,* p. 152. The epigram was composed for a French war memorial, but never used.

29. *Churchill: Four Faces and the Man,* p. 149.

30. *The Second World War* (abr. ed.), p. 957.

31. *Ibid,* p. 958.

32. *Ibid,* p. 973.

33. As if this was not enough, he also published well over four hundred Press articles, in addition to a heavy programme of Parliamentary and extra-parliamentary speeches, and the preparation of six other books.

34. Letter dated 22 September, 1934.

35. A fortunate discovery saved him much unnecessary revision. 'During the Second World War . . . the film director Alexander Korda had bought the film rights of *A History of the English-Speaking Peoples* . . . In the autumn of 1954 the proofs of the version which Korda had bought were found. This was after the corrected proofs of an earlier version of Volumes I and II had already been re-set. This "New Discovery,"

as it was known, was itself then re-set, dated 30 November, 1954 and became the basis of the final version.' (OB, Vol. VIII, p. 1196, n.4.)

36. In a conversation of 19 August, 1953.

37. Churchill, however, had not lost his propensity for wholesale revision. The present writer recalls, while working for Cassell during this period, meeting a senior editor labouring upstairs carrying a pile of paper almost a foot high. Asked if it was the text of Volume II, he replied ruefully, 'No, it's more corrections for Volume I!'

38. Letter dated 23 April, 1956.

39. *Churchill: Four Faces and the Man,* pp. 139-40.

40. *A History of the English-Speaking Peoples,* Vol. I, p. viii.

41. *Ibid,* Vol. I, p. vii.

42. *Ibid,* Vol. IV, p. 304.

43. 'Great Deeds that Gave Us Our Empire,' *Daily Mail,* 24 May 1934.

44. 'Men Who Have Influenced or Impressed Me,' *Strand Magazine,* February, 1931. Reprinted in *Thoughts and Adventures* as 'Personal Contacts'.

Summary

1. For instance, his 1922 prepublication earnings on the first volume of *The World Crisis* (£27,000) would today be worth over £400,000; and his initial outright fee of £20,000 for *A History of the English-Speaking Peoples* (1933) would be worth over £530,000.

   At first glance, these figures might seem illogical, but the decline in monetary values during this century has fluctuated. The figures quoted are based upon information given in *Whitaker's Almanac,* 1990.

2. For example, 'Life under the Microscope' and 'Are there Men in the Moon?'

3. Pound: *op cit,* p. 159.

Appendix I

1. This is surely extremely pretentious. What schoolboy – even an Harrovian in the 1890s – has ever been taught such abstruse details of British history?

2. Letter dated 5 January, 1931. John Hely Owen (1883-1970), after a naval career of 32 years, co-edited four volumes of the Navy Records Society.

3. Charles Carlisle Wood (?-1959). Head of Harrap's Editorial Department and, after his retirement in 1940, Churchill's personal proof-reader. Churchill came to call the process 'wooding'.

4. OB, Vol. V, Comp. Vol. 2, p. 515.

5. Hassall: Edward Marsh, pp. 576-7.

6. Ashley: *Churchill as Historian,* p. 33.

Appendix II

1. Reprinted, with revisions, from Woods: *A Bibliography of the Works of Sir Winston Churchill.*

2. Nowell-Smith: *The House of Cassell,* p. 230. His contention regarding printing times is, of course, hardly logical. Leaving aside the question of differing machine capacities and speeds, the production of the British edition was split up between from three to eight printers and binders, whereas four printers handled both the Houghton Mifflin and the Book of the Month Club editions in the United States.

3. For some reason Cassell switched arbitrarily from alphabetical section-signing to numerical and back again.

4. The Cassell production records are incomplete at this point, and no specific allocation of sections is traceable.

INDEX

180